Millie Robbins
Tales of Love And Hate
in Old San Francisco

MILLIE ROBBINS
Tales of Love and Hate
In Old San Francisco

CHRONICLE BOOKS
San Francisco

To Ted, my husband and Xandra, our daughter

The illustrations of Old San Francisco used on the jacket and section heads are from *San Francisco's Golden Era*, by Lucius Beebe and Charles Clegg. Howell-North Publishers.

Library of Congress Catalog Card No. 70-161031

ISBN O-87701-071-8

Contents

I. Amorous Affairs

II. Mysterious Happenings

III. Rags to Riches

IV. Tragedies

V.   Palatial Places

VI. Unforgettable Characters

I

Amorous Affairs

Amorous Career Led Into Nobility

T HE MATRIMONIAL route for American women into the Almanac de Gotha, the Bible of titled Continentals, isn't always by way of the Social Register. It may be accomplished via the police blotter. This, admittedly, is the hard way, and requires outstanding talents in a specialized field. But it can be done.

Marie Dugas was a luscious, vivacious brunette when she left her native Chicago in the 1880s and came to San Francisco. For reasons best known to herself, she changed her name to Pauline Townsend. But sometimes it was Pauline Davidson and, on occasions, Maude Jackson.

It wasn't long before Pauline acquired a reputation as queen of the night life. Among her admirers were many prominent men of means and she had a high old time for several years.

Then one day Pauline had the misfortune to take up with a disgruntled, miserly chap who reported to the police that she had stolen $130 from his wallet. Actually, this dreary affair turned out to be the most fortunate thing that could have happened to her, for Pauline, to escape the law, headed for Shanghai.

She was an even greater success in the Orient than she had been in San Francisco. Pauline applied herself diligently to her profession, saved her money and amassed a fortune.

She was ready to try her wings in the fashionable purlieus of Europe. In London she met the Baron de Pallandt, a noble Dutchman and an intimate friend of Queen Victoria's high-living son and heir, Edward.

Pauline's abundant charms bowled the Baron over completely. He proposed marriage, something unique in her experience up to this point, and they were wed in 1892.

Thus Miss Townsend—who by this time was calling herself May—annexed a proud title and a secure position in the loftiest of Britain's aristocratic circles.

The marriage lasted a decade. May must have made hay with her spouse's family, too. For her sister-in-law, the Baroness Greenings van Zoellen of The Hague, a former lady-in-waiting to the Dutch queen, left her a large estate.

It must be assumed that the baron had had it by 1903. He offered Marie-Pauline-Maude-May $10,000 for a divorce. She accepted with alacrity, but with the stipulation that she retain the precious title.

Shortly after her divorce, the Baroness reported that she had lost a valuable black pearl at a smart ball given in the British capital. The Mayfair set was highly intrigued when it was discovered during the course of the subsequent publicity that the bauble had been insured in the name of a high-ranking member of the British aristocracy.

The unperturbed Baronness left the embarrassed nobleman to poke under sofas and dig through trashcans and took off with an attractive Frenchman for a tour of the Orient.

In Tokyo she met John D. Kilpatrick, a wealthy New Yorker whose friendship she renewed later in the States. May and Kilpatrick enjoyed a fancy fling around Manhattan for a spell, but eventually they quarreled.

Once more our girl set out for England, her happiest hunting ground. En route she picked up the attractive Frenchman again.

Kilpatrick promptly committed suicide.

May's next important affair was with Dr. Ernest Villiers Appleby, a distinguished savant and former instructor at the University of Minnesota.

His wealthy wife had died a few years before and he then was living in London. He was the son of a former Episcopalian Archdeacon and a relative of the Duke of Clarendon.

But, alas, the professor was no more immune to May's multiple charms than his predecessors had been and he began to lavish luxuries on her.

When Dr. Appleby later hauled May into court in an effort to recoup some of his money, he testified that he'd spent $65,000 on her in less than two years. And that, remember, was when a dollar went a lot farther.

Dr. Appleby had been miffed, it seems, when, following a spat, May had flounced off to New York without him. What really hurt was that she had taken his chauffeur along and not to drive the car.

Mama Wouldn't Let them Marry

THE NAME Dunsmuir means little now but there was a time when it raised eyebrows in San Francisco and children were sent from the room while their elders discussed its owner.

The object of the gossip was Alexander Dunsmuir, the local representative of the flourishing British Columbia coal and shipping empire founded by his father, Robert, who'd migrated from Scotland to the Pacific Coast in 1851 and remained to amass millions.

In the latter part of the '70s Alex, the younger of Robert's two sons, handsome, athletic and in his early 20s, persuaded his father to put him in charge of the newly-opened S.F. office.

He had visited the city several times and found the lively town more to his taste than somewhat-staid Victoria.

Not long after his arrival he became friendly with Waller Wallace, an easy-going blade who was head night usher at the California Theater.

An ardent baseball fan, Wally usually spent his days at the park rooting and reveling with his favorite team.

Soon Wally introduced Alex to his attractive wife, Josephine. The trio got along so well that within a few weeks

Alex moved into the couple's home, which also harbored their two children.

With Wally working nights and at the ballgrounds all day, the inevitable happened: his wife and Alex fell in love, and moreover had plenty of opportunity for dallying.

When Wally got wise to what was going on he decamped, taking the youngsters with him.

Alex began buzzing about socially and also joined a couple of smart men's clubs. Thus he was away from the love nest frequently in the evening. Josephine got lonely and yearned for her offspring, especially her little daughter Edna.

So a deal was made with Wally. He agreed to a cash settlement in exchange for the girl, who later became the well-known actress, Edna Wallace Hopper.

Wally also sued for divorce, thereby clearing the way for his wife to rewed. But Alex was in no hurry.

He knew that his mother—severe, imperious and devout—who wielded great influence with his father, took a dim view of his illicit romance.

He realized that if at this point he married "that woman," as the matriarch Dunsmuir always referred to Josephine, he stood a good chance of losing everything.

So he told his inamorata she'd have to wait a while before ordering the orange blossoms. And she did—for nearly 20 years.

As a result, little Edna was not only shunned by her classmates but even embarrassed by her teachers.

Once, for instance, overhearing an instructor tell another pupil that "Edna's mother was living in sin with a rich Canadian," she rushed home to ask what that meant!

Josephine tried to explain that Alex was prevented temporarily from marrying her, because his mother, an old lady who lived in a castle in Canada, would have him disinherited if he did and they'd have no money to live on.

The excuse must have baffled the child even more.

The strain also began to tell on Alex, who took to tippling. This, of course, only aggravated the sticky situation, and furthermore began to take a toll of his once sturdy Scottish physique.

Thus the years dragged on. Edna grew into a young lady and escaped from the increasingly unhappy menage by going to New York to train for the stage.

Alex's father died in 1889, but left control of the company to his strong-willed wife.

Both Alex and his elder brother, James, tried desperately to buy their mother out—Alex for obvious reasons. As long as she held the reins the threat of disinheritance was ever present.

This arrangement lasted for several years, until finally matriarch Dunsmuir relented and released her holdings.

Toward the end of '98 Alex decided to compensate Josephine for her lengthy devotion by establishing her in a handsome house.

Looking about for a suitable site, he settled on Souther Farm near San Leandro, which, strangely enough, had once been owned by her family.

Alex deeded the estate, more or less completed in 1899 at the cost of some $350,000, to Josephine.

This was about all she was to get for her many years of devotion, though.

On the very day of their long-delayed marriage her lover made out a terse will leaving everything else to his only brother, James, with a verbal understanding that the latter would give Josephine $1000 a month for life.

Alex was 46 when the two sons had finally managed to buy out their mother's controlling interest in the vast British Columbia coal and shipping firm founded by their father.

Then, no longer afraid of being disinherited by his stern,

disapproving mama, Alex was free to make Josephine his wife
and a simple ceremony was performed by a clergyman on
December 21, 1899, in the sitting room of a little hotel in
San Pablo.

A small dinner party at the Oakland home of friends followed and the couple left the next day for a way overdue
honeymoon in New York.

Although the nuptials must have brought Josephine a certain
degree of satisfaction, they were a dismal pair of newlyweds.

For by this time Alex was a confirmed alcoholic. He had
made a tremendous effort to remain sober on his wedding
day, and no liquor was served but it was too late for such
heroics.

On the train he became so ill with withdrawal symptoms
that a supply of whiskey had to be furnished him during the
journey to forestall delirium tremens and he spent the entire
time in his berth.

Josephine's daughter, Edna Wallace Hopper, already a star
on Broadway, was shocked when she saw her at-long-last-legal
step-father. He was so far gone that at first he didn't even
recognize her.

She also was alarmed at the appearance of her obviously
ill mother.

Alex's condition worsened daily. He died in a New York
hospital on New Year's Eve, and his body was sent west to
be buried in Oakland's Mountain View Cemetery.

Josephine, who had become a bride and widow within 40
days, returned to elegant Souther Farm; but, cut adrift and
lonely, she found little pleasure in the lovely estate.

She became irritable and extravagant, dismissed doctors,
quarreled with intimate friends and indulged in senseless
spending sprees.

Poor, pathetic Josephine—once a gay and merry beauty.
She had lived a dubious, backdoor existence for nearly 20 years,

caring for a man who was drinking himself to death, constantly craving matrimony and decent recognition.

Then her hopes were fulfilled only to have them degenerate into a brief and hideous nightmare.

After a couple of unsuccessful operations, she died of cancer on the farm on June 22, 1901, following Alex to the grave by only 18 months.

Poison in the Chocolate Box

NEARLY 70 years ago San Franciscans were treated to the second round of what had been one of the city's most sensational murder cases.

This was when Mrs. Cordelia Botkin, already incarcerated for half a dozen years, was granted a new trial for the murder of both Mrs. John P. Dunning, wife of her erstwhile lover, and Mrs. Joshua A. Deane, who had the misfortune to have been staying with Mrs. Dunning in Dover, Delaware.

The story began one day in 1892 when Dunning, a topflight newspaperman, while bicycling in Golden Gate Park, came across Cordelia seated demurely on a bench and struck up a conversation.

Dunning was smitten with the woman, although she was pushing 40 and more than ten years his senior. An affair ensued that the Spanish American War helped terminate some six years later.

The young man presumably had begun to weary of the liaison, tor when a chance was offered him to cover the conflict he leaped at the assignment. Cordelia wanted to go along and raised a fuss at the train when he departed.

Meanwhile, Mrs. Dunning, a daughter of a former Congressman from Delaware, humilated by her spouse's infidelity, had moved East with their child.

Unwilling to believe that the romance was over, Cordelia apparently came to the conclusion that if Mrs. Dunning were out of the way, her husband would return to the arms of his paramour.

So she sent the wife a box of chocolates laced with arsenic, tucking in a dainty handkerchief as an added fillip, plus a little "note of love." The last proved to be a serious boner. Mmes. Dunning and Deane sampled the candy and died.

The sweetmeats promptly were traced to Mrs. Botkin, thanks to that note, and she was arrested. Dunning was recalled to town for the trial.

Cordelia readily acknowledged knowing Dunning and even supplying him with food and clothing when he needed them. She maintained, however, that "none but the most evil-minded could put a misleading construction on their friendship which was devoid of any impropriety."

While stating coyly that she "lived for the pleasures of the world, solely," Cordelia insisted she couldn't be bothered with murder and, of course, denied buying the bonbons.

But a web of circumstantial evidence inexorably tightened around her. A clerk in a local confectioner's identified Cordelia as the purchaser of the candy, recalling that she asked the box not be filled, as she "wanted to put something else in it"; and another remembered selling her the handkerchief. A drugstore attendant swore he'd sold her the poison and a post office clerk recalled her mailing the package.

The jury took a little more than four hours to come to a verdict of murder in the first degree. Cordelia was sentenced to prison for life and taken to the county jail to await the result of an appeal.

Not long after, the judge who had presided at the trial

boarded a streetcar one afternoon and was flabbergasted to see Cordelia, all gussied-up, seated across the aisle!

It seemed she had so charmed her jailers that she not only had been given a suite instead of a cell and allowed to send out for meals, but was permitted to go on shopping sprees. This caused another flurry of scandal, which in time blew over.

Due to some technicalities, she was granted a new trial in 1904 but was again convicted, and after the 1906 disaster was transferred to San Quentin. Another appeal in 1908 was denied.

Two years later Cordelia, morose and melancholy, died of what was diagnosed as "softening of the brain."

Love Bloomed in Paris

I T WAS in France in 1878 that the 26-year-old Robert Louis Stevenson first met Fanny Osbourne of San Francisco.

The only son of a prosperous Edinburgh civil engineer, he had bitterly disappointed his father by refusing to enter the same profession. He compromised by studying law, but never practiced.

Now he was doing what he'd always wanted to do—writing.

Fanny, some 10 years his senior, was a married woman who already had borne three children.

Nevertheless, she had found time to take painting lessons in the Bay Area, and showed considerable promise.

When her union with Samuel Osbourne soured she packed up her offspring and, accompanied by her sister Nellie, left for Europe to continue her art studies.

Tragedy struck in Antwerp, where one of her little sons died.

The group then proceeded to Paris, and there Fanny made many friends in the flourishing Bohemian colony, which also had attracted Stevenson.

The pair spent many long hours together discussing life, love and literature.

Convinced of the talent of the pale, thin, tubercular young Scot, Fanny encouraged and inspired him.

Perhaps it was inevitable that he should become deeply attached to her.

Three years earlier he had been smitten by an older woman. That passion, however, eventually moderated into a life-long friendship.

At any rate, Fanny, possibly realizing that she lacked sufficient talent, abruptly returned to California. Stevenson was desolate.

Distressed by the gossip of their son's involvement with a married American, his parents had been relieved to learn of her departure.

When he announced his intention of following the charmer, they flatly refused to furnish funds for the trip.

So he saved for nearly three years before accumulating enough to get to this country.

Meanwhile, Fanny had obtained a divorce. She and Stevenson were married by a Presbyterian minister in this city in May, 1880, and a few days later left for the Napa Valley and the sojourn that was to produce "Silverado Squatters."

Then the tide of fortune changed. Stevenson began to find a market for his material.

His parents' attitude softened and the pair, with her son, Lloyd Osbourne, went to visit them.

R. L. S., now in the first flush of fame, was working hard and as his success increased his health worsened.

Following his father's death in 1887 the Stevensons and his mother came to the U. S. heading for warmer climes.

After a short stay at San Francisco's Occidental Hotel, the party sailed for the South Pacific in June 1888 on the Casco, a 94-foot, handsomely-appointed schooner-yacht chartered from its owner, Dr. Samuel Merritt, an eminent physician and former mayor of Oakland.

Dr. Merritt (after whom the lake was named, incidentally) at first had been leery about entrusting his craft to a "peculiar and probably irresponsible literary person."

But the gentle, charming author won him over and he agreed, providing the experienced Captain A. H. Otis be put in command.

Otis' services were engaged for the voyage. But he forbade any discussion of Stevenson's literary works in his presence.

Seems he had read "Treasure Island" and found the seamanship faulty!

A Fair Lady's Method or Madness?

A GREAT deal has been written about Sarah Althea Hill, who claimed to have been married to Senator William Sharon, but another woman made a similar claim on another multi-millionaire, James Fair.

Unlike Sarah, she waited until after his death in December, 1904, when he couldn't talk back. However, some parallels do exist between the two women.

The Fair lady was Mrs. Nettie Craven, a plump, middle-aged school marm, and quite a wheel in local education circles besides. As wily Fair had made provision for $50 in his will for anyone claiming to be his common law wife or any illegitimate offspring, it may be assumed he expected trouble along those lines. After all, his wife had divorced him in 1883 on grounds of "habitual adultery."

It wasn't until after Fair's principal heirs had shown dissatisfaction with the original will (wherein he'd left most of his $40 million or so fortune in trust to them) that Nettie came forward in February, 1895 with one hand-written presumably three days after the first, which gave them their shares outright.

Fair's daughters, Mrs. Hermann Oelrichs and Virginia (not yet Mrs. William K. Vanderbilt Jr.), and his surviving son, Charles, were jubilant. This gave rise to rumors that they'd made some sort of a financial deal with Nettie. But that hardly seemed likely and their joy turned to consternation as Mrs. Craven proceeded to dig more documents out of her trunk.

For she also produced deeds purportedly giving her two pieces of valuable San Francisco real estate and more important—as Sarah had done—a marriage contract.

By this time calling herself Mrs. Craven-Fair, Nettie asked for a third of the estate.

There was plenty of evidence of hanky-panky between the Comstock tycoon and the ambitious dynamic woman who heretofore had been so good at keeping secrets.

Nettie hailed from Illinois and had received her teaching credentials, it's said, at the tender age of 14. Her first major post had been at Alameda High School where she was assistant to the principal, Andrew Fuller Craven, and soon married her boss.

But Nettie proved to be too much for the mild-mannered professor, or perhaps he wasn't enough for her. In any event, they were divorced.

Our girl then came to San Francisco, served as the principal of one small school and subsequently was promoted to the head of the far larger Mission Grammar School, which had a student body of around 1000. She was an able but not overly popular administrator.

Just where or when busy Nettie caught up with crafty, Slippery Jim, never one to crave education or refinement, isn't clear.

When the case came to trial, Nettie insisted that although Fair had loved her deeply and long, he wanted to keep their union quiet, and had given her the marriage contract for protection. Moreover, she maintained that in a burst of ardor he had agreed to a wedding ceremony over which a justice of the peace in Sausalito had officiated.

This character, a former streetcar motorman, was brought to the stand and at first testified for Nettie but later contradicted himself.

In the end Nettie, like Sarah, got nowhere. When her claims were thrown out of court she left San Francisco forever and was in Iowa when last heard from.

As with Sarah, who died in the State hospital at Stockton, Nettie, too, spent her last days in a mental institution.

Although some $2 million had been spread around among lawyers after Mrs. Nettie Craven produced a marriage contract and asked for, but didn't get, a third of the huge estate, there still was plenty of money left.

So an assortment of others came forward, asserting various types of relationships in hope of snagging a slice of the enormous pie.

The most prominent of these was Phoebe Couzins, a world-renowned advocate of women's rights, said to be the first female attorney in the Nation and the first woman to hold the office of U.S. marshal.

While in San Francisco on a lecture tour she confided to the press that she had been engaged to Fair at the time of his death. Their courtship had budded in Chicago, but it had been a frustrating one, she said, as the aging multimillionaire's nurse, two secretaries and a nephew constantly ran interference to keep them apart. Nevertheless, they had managed a few brief moments together and he'd asked her to be his wife.

She also accused the watchdogs of taking him out of a warm bed on a cold day for a long, lakefront drive in an open carriage. When, as might be expected, he contracted pneumonia, she was refused any opportunity to visit him and all communications were intercepted. After this admission, her audiences on the Coast were sell-outs.

Sarah Gamble, a 19-year-old girl, also maintained she was Fair's fiancee. Pretty Sarah sold flowers from a stand in front of a Los Angeles hotel, and Fair had been among her best customers. He frequently took her for buggy rides, too, and in the course of one trip proposed and was apparently accepted.

An Oakland girl in her 20s presented herself as a natural daughter and asked for a quarter of the fortune. A young man who called himself James Fair Stevens said he was the result of a romance in Virginia City between his mother and the Comstock nabob prior to the latter's divorce.

And so it went for the next 27 years, as the dispute went on.

Most of this effort appears to have been useless, but claimants apparently worked on the nothing ventured, nothing gained theory.

The lengthy litigation finally was closed in March, 1922, when a settlement was made with Mrs. Mary Jane Lundy on behalf of her dead sister, Elisa Ann Fair, a niece of the tycoon.

It was for a piddling $8500.

Playing House Didn't Pay Off

THE LADY's true given name was Lydia M. Valencia, and it was said (but not substantiated) that she stemmed from the pioneer Spanish-California family for whom Valencia street was christened.

The story goes that due to her parents' financial difficulties she had quit school at an early age and became a professional dancer.

What dancing she may have done must have been in the seamier sections of town, as around the turn of the century she was well known as Dodie, the toast of the Barbary Coast.

A dark-eyed brunette, her somewhat demure appearance belied her activities.

She probably never was mentioned in polite mixed company until 1905, when she started to play house with David Jennings Baird.

(Some accounts have it that David took over where his brother Miles left off.)

In any event the Baird family was highly respectable, socially prominent and rich, so David's association with the notorious Dodie was as embarrassing as it was irritating.

The couple lived together devotedly and openly for three years.

They never got around to having the union legalized, although occasionally they made a few abortive attempts to do so.

Once, for instance, they started out to get married in Redwood City. But so often did they refresh themselves at roadhouses en route that they weren't able to reach their destination.

Nevertheless, three weeks before a son was born to her in 1906, David gave Dodie a wedding ring and to her dying day she called herself Mrs. Baird.

Baird died suddenly in 1908, leaving an estate variously estimated as between $250,000 and $1 million.

In his will, drawn up five years earlier, he left everything to his mother and sister. Not a red cent for Dodie or the baby, who weren't even mentioned.

The following month Dodie filed suit to establish the paternity of David, Jr. and obtain a settlement for him.

She maintained that Baird had acknowledged the boy as his son in the presence of several witnesses, had brought him toys and taught him games.

Moreover, she produced a birth certificate listing him as the father and a good deal of other evidence.

In 1909, only a few months after Baird's death, Dodie became a bride at last.

Her husband was another rich youth, James Clay Dunphy, the son of a wealthy cattleman. He had just been sprung from a marriage due to the fact that his erstwhile wife had not been legally severed from her former spouse.

It may be assumed that Dunphy, perhaps desolate over the break-up of his matrimonial lark, and Dodie, still mourning the death of her paramour, had found consolation in each other.

Accompanied by another couple, they arrived at their destination late at night. Nevertheless, Dodie was sober enough to see that a county clerk was rousted out of bed to produce a license and an obliging justice of the peace performed the ceremony in a suite they'd engaged in a local hotel.

Once the knot was tied though, the foursome motored back to San Francisco where the wedding celebration was continued.

In fact the festivities went on for four days—at the end of which Dunphy pulled himself together and filed for annulment!

His petition was quickly granted. The judge ruled that the marriage had been contracted "during a period of bibulous exuberance" as "both parties had consumed a large load of spirituous liquor en route."

Dodie couldn't have cared much as she didn't put up a fight.

She had more important things on her mind, anyhow, such as the battle to establish the paternity of her son.

This was the beginning of what has been called the longest legal contest of its kind ever staged in local courts. It went on for the next 20 years!

Twice juries ruled in Dodie's favor, only to have the decision set aside by the State Supreme Court. Still she fought on as her son grew into manhood.

She was preparing to file her fourth suit against the Bairds in 1929 when 23-year-old David, Jr., soloing in a plane near the old Alameda airport, crashed and burned to death.

It was all over for Dodie, who faded out of the news.

One day late in 1948 a sick old lady entered St. Francis Hospital—was generally agreeable, but refused to give attendants her age.

There she died in November. The funeral notice read "Lydia Valencia Baird, beloved wife of the late David Jennings Baird."

She used the name she had no right to and one she never was able to obtain legally for her beloved only son.

The Socialite and the . . . Lady?

ALLAN ST. JOHN BOWIE was the seventh of nine children born to the distinguished Dr. Augustus J. Bowie, member of an old, respected Maryland family and a Navy physician who came to San Francisco in 1849.

Dr. Bowie, a brilliant surgeon as well as a classical scholar and expert linguist, amassed a large fortune, mostly in real estate.

It's just as well that he didn't live to see the mess in which Allan became embroiled around the turn of the century with the notorious Jessie Hayman, one of the city's most renowned madams.

Jessie had a lot going for her. Redheaded, with a slim, trim figure, she dressed expensively and well. Besides, she had brains, could be a charming companion and wisely invested the money that rolled in.

Furthermore, she ran a tight ship, permitting no rowdiness or foul language on the part of patrons or playmates in her elegantly operated establishments.

She insisted that every girl have a stylish wardrobe, passed on by Jessie herself, *and* a maid, whose wages were taken out of the girl's earnings.

Unlike most of her counterparts, she served food and drink, and she'd countenance no quibbling about prices.

In short, Jessie catered to the carriage trade, which undoubtedly accounts for her meeting with Allan St. John, a prominent clubman and dashing bachelor in his early 40s, who was president of the Western Light and Power Company.

Bowie found Jessie more tasty than any of the debutantes who'd been dangled before him and a warm relationship developed between the two. It became public knowledge and was Topic A from the Tenderloin's parlor houses to the drawing rooms of Pacific Heights.

Now, Jessie knew men well, and up to this point had taken a dim view of marriage.

With the advent of Allan, however, her perspective changed. She began to covet a plain band under the handsome diamond rings she wore on the fourth finger of her left hand.

Why not? After all, the woman she'd first worked for in San Francisco had retired to marry a lumberman, and was accepted by Peninsula Society.

She felt she could hold her own with the best of them. Moreover, she could even furnish a sizable dowry, what with all her bonds, securities and real estate holdings, not to mention money in the bank.

Bowie, though, was content with the way things were.

Time marched on and Bowie still made no move toward matrimony:

In 1917, when she was pushing 50, Jessie had a comfortable income from shrewd investments. So she kissed the girls goodby, closed shop and went to live quietly with a devoted companion-maid and a couple of cats. It wasn't an exciting life.

Several years later she packed a wardrobe of fashionable clothes and her best jewels and set off alone on an extensive world junket. She toured the Orient, India, Egypt and the Continent for three months, finally arriving in London where she settled down for a while.

Proving perhaps that she still harbored hope—or maybe it was just habit—she registered at a smart hotel as Mrs. Jessie May Bowie. This act subsequently was to embarrass her lover.

Jessie had been conducting herself with great decorum which, oddly enough, only served to attract attention. Although she was always magnificently dressed and bejeweled, the hotel staff thought it strange that she had no friends, nor made any.

For example, she was always alone at meals.

Then one night in the spring of 1923 she didn't appear in the dining room. The next morning a maid, entering her suite, found her seated in a chair, wearing evening clothes.

Jessie had been dead for several hours.

The small obit that appeared in a London paper was picked up by an alert newspaper correspondent who wired the item to San Francisco, including the sentence: "Mrs. Bowie is thought to be the wife of San Francisco millionaire Allan St. John Bowie."

They thought wrong.

Jessie's body was shipped home for burial.

Her estate included, besides lots of real estate, stocks, bonds and oil leases in Louisiana.

It was divvied up among a pack of nieces and nephews, but $1000 had been allotted for the upkeep of her two tabbies.

In 1926 Bowie married for the first time. He gave his age as 54 (shaving truth by a dozen years). His bride, Anita Imelda Hughes, was half his age.

It was a stormy marriage. Within nine years they separated, and Anita Imelda sailed off to the Orient with another man.

During the summer of 1937 Bowie was taken seriously ill. His wife (her status became a matter of doubt) rushed to his side and stayed there until the end. This despite the fact that she had divorced him in Mexico and married her traveling companion!

Bowie died at 77 early the next year and started a fight among his relatives by leaving all his money to Anita Imelda. Had Jessie been around she would have laughed—hollowly.

A Gal, a Guy, and a Gun

THE MOST famous incident to occur on a San Francisco ferryboat took place back in 1870, shortly after the completion of the transcontinental railroad necessitated putting them on regular schedules.

It was a murder with an all-star cast.

Taking the male lead was Alexander Parker Crittenden, an affluent and highly respected citizen with the world for his oyster. He ran with the South Park set, than which there was nothing more select in that day. All the transplanted Southern aristocrats had their genteel mansions around the oval.

Crittenden had graduated from West Point with both Beauregard and Sherman. He was one of the most celebrated lawyers in the State, a bright beacon not only at the bar but in many another important professional group. Courtly and handsome, he was the father of seven children and even had a few grandchildren.

Co-starred with him was Mrs. Laura D. Fair, at least 25 years his junior. She was blonde (once billed on the stage as California's first bobbed-haired actress), with limpid eyes in a heart-shaped face. But she was no ingenue. Alluring Laura had been married twice—twice widowed, once by suicide, and once divorced. She was not of the South Park gentry either.

Laura and Crittenden first met when she was running a boarding house at Virginia City, where he was a guest. She was a Southern sympathizer. During the Civil War, when her business partner raised the Stars and Stripes over their establishment, she resented the gesture so intensely that she emphasized her point with a near-fatal slug. Crittenden argued her case and she was acquitted.

Thereafter they got along like yams and ham. The shooting episode should have warned Crittenden that the lady could be fast with a firearm. But love is notoriously myopic.

Pretending to be a widower, Crittenden became betrothed to Laura. It took her a year to find out that he had a wife, but she forgave the deception when he promised to divorce his helpmate.

Laura had patience. She continued to be understanding for the next six years. Then one day her patience came to an abrupt end and she shot Crittenden before the horrified eyes of his wife.

The murder of the eminent barrister and society-man-about-town by his paramour kept hundreds of citizens in absorbing conversation for years.

Clergymen thundered from their pulpits on sacred vs. profane love, newspapers carried reams of editorials, and the public savored each delicious detail.

Laura testified at her trial that her lover had promised once again to ask his wife for a divorce as soon as that unsuspecting lady arrived at the Oakland Mole following a trip to the East. He then would return immediately to Laura and tell her how Mrs. Crittenden had taken the bad tidings.

But after six years of Crittenden's stalling, Laura hadn't trusted her boy and had followed him. She watched the Crittendens' affectionate meeting, saw them board the ferryboat *El Capitan* and with some of their seven children form a happy family group on the upper deck.

Laura heard Mrs. Crittenden's "peculiar and disagreeable voice" (as she called it) babble merrily on and figured that once again she had been deceived. He hadn't intended to make an honest woman of her after all.

But Mrs. Fair was prepared. She walked up close and let him have one well-aimed slug from her "fourshooter" in the chest.

"I did it and I'm glad," said Laura to the arresting officers. "He ruined me."

Crittenden died in great agony at his home 48 hours later. He was given one of the largest and most impressive funerals ever held in San Francisco. Federal, State, county and municipal courts adjourned out of respect.

Laura's trial was a rouser from start to finish. Hundreds of Crittenden's love letters, gushing with ardor and sentimentality, were introduced. Laura swore that her brief marriage to another man in the middle of the Crittenden idyll was only a heroic but futile attempt to wash the Southern gentleman out of her hair. Laura's defense was emotional insanity.

The jurors were out only a snappy 40 minutes before they returned with the verdict: guilty of murder in the first degree. Laura was condemned to be hanged—the first woman in California to receive the death sentence. The judge had tears in his eyes as he pronounced it and many another in the jammed courtroom wept, too.

But there was no need to build the gallows yet.

Her lawyers appealed to the Supreme Court and there was a stay of execution. Almost two years later her case came to trial again. This time 12 gallant gentlemen acquitted her!

Laura lived to the ripe age of 82. She died alone in 1919 in a little house way out on Market Street.

The Marrying Millionaire

T HERE's no indication that Lucian H. Sly ever entertained any notion of changing his unfortunate, Dickensian name.

Had he switched to some more righteous sounding tag, such as "Noble" or "Sterling," it's conceivable that the course of his life could have been altered.

Sly made a modest fortune in Alaska before coming to San Francisco in the '90s and investing in real estate. At the time of the 1906 disaster he owned several first-rate apartment buildings here and already was rated a millionaire.

The fire destroyed the Leland Stanford mansion at California and Powell streets and the following year Sly bought the property. On it he erected the Stanford Court Apartments, and also built several other impressive multiple dwellings in the downtown area.

At one point he was reported to have had the largest income of any apartment-building owner in the State.

However, Sly must have been a contentious character, for he constantly was embroiled in litigation of one sort or another.

He battled with trade unions and labor in general. In 1915 a group of firms sued him for non-payment of $80,000 for material that had gone into the construction of the Nob Hill building.

That year, also, he was hauled into court on the complaint of Robert W. Shingle, a prominent Honolulu banker. The Shingles, with their five children under the age of six, had leased a Stanford Court apartment for a couple of months.

Maintaining the youngsters made too much noise, Sly ordered the family to shift to a suite of rooms on the upper floor. When they didn't move fast enough, he dropped in and told them they had exactly one minute before he would cut off utilities.

Shingle won a restraining order preventing eviction.

But it was Sly's matrimonial meanderings, begun when he was pushing 60, that furnished most of the gossip and kept him in the local press for 15 years or so.

In March, 1919, he divorced his first wife and the following May married Mrs. Leda Carnahan, a well-known local amateur soprano. This union soured almost before the wedding bells stopped ringing.

Leda filed suit for divorce that July, charging that her spouse was extremely suspicious and jealous of her music teacher Nino Marcelli, an Oakland orchestra conductor.

He had accused her of cutting their honeymoon short and rushing back to the Bay Area in order to be with the musician.

"If she should run away with Marcelli," Sly is reported to have told friends, "she would be on the rocks in two months and come crawling back to me on her belly."

This caused the lady great anguish and humiliation and probably shook up Nino, too.

Exit Leda with her divorce—and a settlement besides.

Sly next espoused Lottie Thompson in Sacramento on Dec. 3, 1921, and they went off on an extended European honeymoon. But as soon as they were back in New York he wanted out.

"Thank goodness we have reached land. Now I can get rid of you," he said to Lottie in the presence of witnesses.

He left for San Francisco alone, telling her to stay where she was. Nevertheless, Lottie followed the next day, only to find herself locked out of their town house here.

So she went to their country home at Santa Cruz. Whereupon he promptly sold the place and she was without a roof. In January, 1924, Lottie got her divorce and a lot more—including one of Sly's most lucrative apartment houses and a hefty cash settlement.

That hurt, and Sly vowed before anyone who'd listen that he'd never marry again. He did, though, in little over a year. Mrs. Coral Wreath Hargrove, billed as a society matron from Modesto, became his fourth sparring partner in February, 1925.

A few years later, he suggested she take a trip. Upon returning, Coral found her door bolted. Moreover, Sly once again in the divorce court, charged desertion! Coral counter-sued, giving the same reason, and won.

This apparently marked the end of Sly's rocky marital march. For when he died at 82 in 1944, there was no widow to mourn him.

The Gould's Marital Mix-ups

KATHERINE CLEMMONS began her career with Shakespearean roles in San Francisco, switched to performing with Buffalo Bill, then managed to meet and marry Howard, son of tycoon Jay Gould.

Thereupon she retired from the stage but not, as it turned out, from the spotlight.

Howard apparently had a preference for theatrical over social women, and he was engaged to an actress whom he promptly ditched when Katherine came along.

He wooed the maid from the Bay Area for four years before she consented to become his bride in 1893.

Katherine stemmed from a modest middle-class local family. (Her sister ran a curio shop in Chinatown here.) With her marriage she moved into the big time.

The senior Goulds might not have rolled out a gilded welcome mat for their new daughter-in-law but, as Howard had a fat purse of his own, this didn't much matter. (He left $60 million when he died at 88.)

When the couple weren't cruising about the world on their palatial yacht, the *Niagara*—frequently escorted by assorted crowned heads—they were entertaining lavishly in Castle Gould, their magnificent Long Island residence, a reasonable replica of Kilkenny Castle in Ireland.

For a few years it was smooth, super-sailing. Then in 1908 Gould decided he'd had enough of Katherine and took steps to get rid of her.

The whole miserable business landed in court, with Gould lashing out in all directions.

He charged that his wife was a falling-down lush who drank her way through the day beginning with pre-breakfast cocktails.

He also accused her of infidelity, naming Buffalo Bill as an old flame and Western actor Dustin Farnum as a new one.

A parade of witnesses with pro and con convictions trooped through the New York courtroom, providing the Nation's press with columns of copy.

But in the end Katherine was completely vindicated, and was awarded $36,000 a year alimony and valuable property.

Mr. Farnum, by the way, had pooh-poohed any romantic interest in Katherine, concluding with this ungallant clincher: "Why, she was an established actress when I was a boy."

Now let's consider Howard's younger brother, Frank, whose marriage to Florence Lacaze, a San Franciscan, was enduring and presumably happy.

But before Frank and Florence got together, he had worked his way through two other wives.

Helen Kelly, a 16-year-old just out of a convent, became the first Mrs. Frank in 1901. Charging misconduct, she sued him eight years (and two children) later.

The following year in Paris he married Edith Kelly, a British showgirl.

In the interim, a dancer named Bessie De Voe sued him for breach of promise. To bolster her case, Bessie had made public some of his incendiary love letters.

This so embarrassed and humiliated their writer that he
fled to Europe to remain an expatriate for the remainder of
his life.

Enter Florence, beautiful and chic.

She was born to parents of French extraction, attended
school in Marin and then studied and acted abroad.

She also experienced a brief matrimonial interlude with
Henry Chittenden Heynemann, a San Francisco architect
whose bride she became in Spain in 1914. The pair returned
to the United States and split up within a couple of years.

While Frank still was trying to get his problems with Edith
ironed out, Florence and her mother, Mrs. Bertha Lacaze,
whiled away the time in Paris selecting an elaborate trousseau
and making plans to do over Gould's handsome house. Finally
the path was cleared for them to wed in 1923.

Gould is credited with having turned the sleepy little community of Juan-les-Pins on the Riviera into a glittering resort
town and wound up virtually owning the place.

In subsequent years his income from hotels, restaurants and
gambling casinos was believed to be in excess of $150,000
a day, and upon his death in 1956 his estate was estimated
at somewhere between $100 and $150 million.

The widow Florence brought Frank Gould's body to this
country for burial. Although he had lived in France for over
46 years, he'd never relinquished his American citizenship.

He Got a Wife He Didn't Want

AMONG the more celebrated cases in San Francisco's history was that involving multimillionaire Senator William Sharon; his beautiful mistress, Sarah Althea Hill; her swashbuckling suitor, David S. Terry, and the city's most sinister figure, Mammy Pleasant.

For a quick recap:

Sarah arrived, presumably from the Deep South, about 1870, sought out Sharon for "advice" and became his mistress. He was around 60 and she young enough to be his daughter. When he tried to oust her she filed suit for "divorce" and asked for a division of community property. Everybody laughed (except her own lawyer, who was bewildered) until she dramatically drew a document from her bosom. This proved to be a "marriage contract" signed by the Senator.

Sharon admitted that it was his signature all right. He had signed a blank paper once, he said, because Sarah had asked for his autograph! So his startled legal battery began to oil up their big guns. They even accused Sarah and Mammy Pleasant of indulging in voodoo.

It is thought that Mammy bolstered Sarah with thousands of dollars, too.

While all of this was keeping the populace enthralled, a lawyer named David S. Terry strolled into court to see some of the fireworks at first hand. Charmed by the comely Sarah, he decided to enter the fray on her side. Terry was an adventurous hothead with a colorful past. He had been a brigadier general in the Confederate army, a justice of California's Supreme Court and had fought a duel with and killed Senator David C. Broderick at Lake Merced. He fell madly in love with Sarah.

After 15 months of litigation, a decision was rendered on Christmas Eve in 1885. Sarah was adjudged Sharon's common-law wife and the property division was ordered. The following month she and Terry were married. Shortly after, the Federal Circuit Court reversed the decision. Then Sharon died.

The case dragged on into higher courts with more decisions and reversals and ended when Justice Stephen Field ruled against Althea. Terry threatened to kill him and the frightened Field hired a bodyguard.

Then fate took a hand in the game. Sarah and Terry, while changing trains at Lathrop near Tracy, went into the railroad lunchroom. Field and his bodyguard, David Nagle, already were there. The unarmed Terry walked over and slapped Field's face, whereupon Nagle shot Terry dead.

The bullet that killed her husband also shattered Sarah's mind. Not long after, she was found wandering in a hysterical daze on Kearny street near Sutter. She was admitted to the Stockton State Hospital for the insane in 1892 to remain for 45 years happily living the illusion, according to the superintendent of the institution, that she had wealth and position. When she died at a ripe 86 in 1937, she was buried in a plot next to Judge Terry's in a Stockton cemetery.

An Affair Remembered

MRS. WILLIAM C. RALSTON's infatuation for John A. Chandor and her manner of squandering money following her banker husband's death in 1875 had been chewed over with consternation in social circles at home and abroad for a long time.

The gossip moved into the open when she demanded that her uncle, Colonel J. D. Fry, who'd been administering her estate, "reconvey her property and surrender her trust." This he did reluctantly.

It seems that within a year she had not only dissipated her ample income but a large portion of the principal as well and now wanted to convert the remainder into accessible cash.

Responsible for the move, it was said, was her constant companion, Chandor.

The impressionable Mrs. Ralston, then 40 years old, had met Chandor on the steamer in 1877 when she sailed for the Continent with her two sons, planning to live quietly and give the boys a European education.

He was about 33, suave, seemingly well-educated and of that "prepossessing appearance calculated to give him unlimited success with the fair sex."

He maintained he was the son of an American contractor in St. Petersburg. It subsequently developed that his father, Lassallo Chandor, was a notorious confidence man.

She first believed the rascal to be single but later learned he was estranged from a wife in New York.

At any rate, Mrs. Ralston bought an expensive house in Paris, where Chandor joined her.

The report that the pair was to be married did not do much to soften the criticism for the simple reason that there was a mystery about Chandor which the most industrious seeker after the truth could not penetrate.

When Mrs. Ralston returned to California to acquire more funds, Chandor accompanied her only as far as Colorado where it was rumored he hoped to get a divorce, but didn't.

Her business here completed, Mrs. Ralston met Chandor and proceeded to Niagara Falls.

For a period, the gossips of the Falls were teeming with stories of the extravagance and dissipation of the California widow and her companion, whose relationship was not clearly understood.

After Niagara Mrs. Ralston stayed at a fashionable New York hotel, where she was joined by her two daughters before again sailing for Europe. Chandor stayed with his wife. Then he, too, departed—on the same ship. Forty years of silence followed, as far as the press was concerned.

"The news of her death was virtually the first heard of her in half a century—coming to old-timers like a voice from the far past."

Thus read a newspaper account of the demise on November 30, 1929, of the 92-year-old widow of William C. Ralston.

The story was not entirely accurate.

An enterprising reporter on the *Auburn Daily Journal* had located Mrs. Ralston in 1918 but made nothing much of the story.

"She maintains her residence in a handsome Georgetown area," according to the brief article published in that paper on January 3 that year. "She usually winters at her home but will spend the next few months at Placerville.

"Mrs. Ralston became utterly tired of metropolitan life and went to the Sierra. Here she enjoys the beautiful mountains and her books."

A quiet life in the Sierra was a long, long way from Paris and her wildly romantic episode with Chandor.

After he helped her dissipate a fortune of some $250,000, had the inevitable happened? Did the youthful, personable Chandor desert her soon after the money was gone, leaving in hot pursuit of some other wealthy widow? Or to return to his wife?

The story of her infatuation and extravagances which had so intrigued her contemporaries was forgotten by 1929.

"What happened to one of San Francisco's most queenly hostesses after her husband died was not generally known," read the obituary.

"Most assumed she had followed him to the grave."

(Not for 54 years she didn't!)

"They did not know that the woman whose presence was a necessary grace to any noteworthy function of pioneer aristocracy salvaged what she could from the wreck" (of the Bank of California etc.) "and retired into the Sierra vastness."

(Not until after she'd had a bang-up fling in New York and Paris she didn't.)

"And there she lived as a virtual recluse for three—maybe four—decades. To Georgetown in the high Sierra she went, no one knows how many years ago, and there lived adjacent to the Ralston mine her sons William and Samuel were developing for a while.

"Her return to the city over whose elite she once reigned was unheralded, unrecorded."

Mrs. Ralston died in her Pacific avenue apartment and was buried beside her husband in Cypress Lawn Cemetery.

But nobody knows whatever became of Chandor.

Frankie and Tessie Were Lovers

T ESSIE WALL was Queen of the Tenderloin around the turn of the century and after.

Amazingly enough, Tessie, whose famous bordello used to be on O'Farrell street, was highly intrigued by society. It is said that she pored over the social columns in all of the newspapers, although she didn't know any of the women whose names appeared. She did know many of the men, however.

She also had a hankering for the same sort of possessions that the social folk liked—diamonds, oil paintings, valuable rugs, silver and china. When she died in the early thirties, among the articles of her estate auctioned off was a crimson Oriental rug that had been in the kitchen of her last home on 18th street. There also was a gold dinner service as well as a handsome green and gold one which had been made expressly for William Rockefeller and was embossed with his initials.

But most of all Tessie yearned to attend a top grade social affair—especially a Mardi Gras Ball. They say she did once, too, managing to secure an invitation from an important politico. Although her name was not used in the guest list printed

after the event, she managed to let the populace know she
had realized her ambition by losing a diamond brooch somewhere between O'Farrell street and the place where the ball
was held. This piece of news was duly recorded and the town
snickered.

Tessie's love affair with Frank Daroux, the handsome dashing gambler and political boss, was definitely in "Frankie and
Johnnie" tradition. She was mad about the guy and remained
that way all of her life. They had married at a civil ceremony
in Philadelphia but three years later had the union sanctified
in San Francisco by a gentleman of the cloth. At their belated
wedding breakfast the 100 guests consumed 80 cases of champagne, which one mathematically-minded reporter broke
down to 960 bottles or 240 gallons. Tessie's only regret was
that she couldn't have a 100-piece brass band at the church.

It was when Frank suggested that she change her mode
of life and become a Peninsula housewife that Tessie made
her historic pronouncement: "I'd rather be an electric pole
on Powell street than own all of San Mateo county."

Within a few years, Frank tired of his voluptuous blonde
wife and sued for divorce. Tessie fought the action like a
tigress. She tried to dissect herself with a carving knife, created
a stir in judicial circles by screaming that Frank maintained
he had the Supreme Court in the palm of his sticky hand,
and hauled Mary C. Lund, the "other" woman, into court.
But Frank got his divorce, anyway.

Six months later Tessie caught up with him on Powell street.
They quarreled bitterly as they entered Anna lane (off Ellis).
She whipped out a gun and shot him three times, twice in
the back, but fortunately not fatally. Sobbing hysterically, Tess
followed Frank to the hospital, solicitously inquiring after his
welfare at frequent intervals.

"I shot him because I love him. Frank still belongs to me,"
she confided to everyone within earshot.

II

Mysterious Happenings

The Mystery of the Unfinished House

THE ZANY construction of Sarah L. Winchester's "House of Mystery" four miles west of San Jose is familiar to almost everyone in those parts, not to mention countless tourists.

The widowed multimillionairess acquired it when it was a 17-room dwelling in the late '80s or early '90s. Thereafter she kept a corps of skilled artisans—frequently 30 at a time— employed building, unbuilding and rebuilding for 36 years until the house had reached 160 rooms.

Included are more than a thousand doors and windows— many leading into blank walls; 47 fireplaces, a number with no chimneys; 40 staircases, most leading nowhere; 13 bathrooms, some with glass doors; secret passageways and trap doors. The whole Charles Addams bit.

After the water pipes had frozen, one winter not long ago, a dozen hitherto unknown faucets in inaccessible places were discovered.

There is an opulent ballroom where no one of this world at any rate ever has danced, and closets in which no clothes ever could have hung as they open into space

That she planned to go on constructing is evident by the stacks of fine wood, beautiful tiles, screening and other material found in an out-building at Llanada Villa, as it was called, at the time of her death in 1922.

But one of the mysteries never touched upon in the tangled tales of lore and legend is why she concentrated on this particular house when she owned other pieces of property on the peninsula.

Following the death of her beloved husband, William Wirth Winchester, scion of Oliver Fisher Winchester, founder of the repeating arms company that bore his name, and their young son, she sought refuge from her great grief in spiritualism.

The disembodied, so they say, told her that she would live as long as she continued building. But why did she not build elsewhere and to better purpose?

Around the turn of the century she'd bought some 98 acres in Burlingame, most of it marshland—and at one point apparently expected to erect a house there.

At the foot of Oak Grove avenue, near Francis Carolan's onetime polo field, Mrs. Winchester had constructed a costly concrete sea wall, a network of canals and flood gates, and a boathouse. Then the work abruptly stopped.

It was rumored that Mrs. Winchester probably would maintain a fleet of yachts and boats to make their way along the watery paths.

Presumably the house was to have been erected on a huge mound of soil thus commanding a view of the complicated ditch system.

Then she had several choice acres in Atherton, part of property that once had belonged to the prominent pioneer Faxon Dean Atherton and surrounded by lovely estates. On it was an impressive abode of Spanish architecture, the upper story ornamented with arched balconies.

Whether she ever lived there is a matter for conjecture as the petite Mrs. Winchester (she was less than 5 feet tall) was a recluse who shunned contact with her fellow man.

This place she sold in 1911 reportedly for $200,000 to Mrs. Delia Fleishhacker, grandmother of Mortimer Fleishhacker, Jr.

There was a handsome piece of land near Belmont that she owned, too, and for a while speculation had it that she would build there but nothing came of that either.

The story goes that although she refused to see visitors—Harry Houdini once called and found her "out"—she lived, sometimes with a secretary, in luxury attended by a staff of loyal, close-mouthed Oriental servants.

She'd dine off gold plate, for instance, after which the service immediately was stashed away in vaults.

Bloodhounds roamed the grounds to discourage the curious.

It's believed that she had inherited about $20 million from her spouse. Her fortune, however, eventually dwindled to $4 million. (Building costs were high even then.)

The Sobbing Ghost

ONE OF the few ghosts with a social aura we've ever heard about is a hitch-hiking young lady who occasionally flags down motorists in Oakland's downtown section and in desperate tones asks to be driven to an address in Berkeley. The story always is the same, except that often the locale changes slightly. She climbs into the rear seat and sobs quietly. The embarrassed driver respects her privacy and doesn't turn around until he reaches the designated address. When he does, she has vanished.

Curious, he rings the doorbell of a large and charming house and tells his tale to the sad-faced woman who answers the door. She isn't surprised.

"Yes, I know," she says wearily. "That's my daughter. Several years ago en route back from a ball she was killed on the corner of 14th and Broadway. She has been trying to get home ever since."

A few stories have her appearing near Hayward. As a matter of fact, several motorists spotted a luminous figure on a railroad trestle near Hayward five or six years ago. They notified the Alameda county sheriff's office. Investigation proved that all that glows is not ectoplasm. A boy from one of the nearby ranches just wanted to help the legend along and turned up at midnight wearing a white garment daubed with phosphorescent paint.

There was a ghost in Golden Gate Park once, too, or so insisted a party that was motoring many years past along the South drive during the early morning hours. The driver of the car was one Arthur Pigeon, a solid citizen—in fact, a cement merchant. He was returning with several women after a gay evening at the beach resorts. All of the terrified group maintained stoutly that they had seen the same thing. What's more, they were able to furnish details.

The specter was tall and thin, they said, dressed in white, had long, fair hair and was barefooted. It stood in front of a cypress tree with arms extended as though trying to stop the vehicle. No one, however, noticed the face.

The ladies shrieked and the driver pushed down hard on the throttle. About half a mile on, a cruising policeman caught up with the speeding automobile and must have been considerably impressed to discover that the occupants were quaking with fright. When he was told by Pigeon that they were exceeding the speed limit because they had just seen a ghost, the cop undoubtedly felt grudging admiration for the novelty of their excuse. He suggested quietly but firmly that they all go back and point out the supernatural visitor to him.

The frightened women flatly refused, however. So they got out and huddled together by the roadside while Pigeon and the officer slowly drove back to the spot. Although Pigeon was certain that he had found the exact tree, there wasn't the ghost of a ghost in sight.

Of course not. Daylight was breaking and everyone knows that phantoms fade at dawn.

Death Revealed a Do-Gooder's Secret

I T ALL seems a trifle odd, and many questions must remain unanswered, but here's the story anyway.

Around 8 o'clock on a September evening in 1936, a little old man collapsed, fell to the pavement at the corner of Post and Franklin streets, and was taken to St. Francis Hospital.

This was Jack Bee Garland, a familiar figure to hundreds around town.

Wearing a cheap blue suit, shoes that seemed too large for him and a hat pulled down over his thin, almost childlike face, he had roamed the streets at night for years, doling out coins to the hungry, the sick and the destitute.

Not that he ever had much money himself. His home was a dismal room located on Taylor street.

Doctors were amazed to discover that 67-year-old "Mr. Garland"—who died a few hours after being picked up—was a woman.

Before dying, she had murmured the names of the only people who knew her secret—a man and a woman in this city and a sister who lived in Los Angeles.

Jack Garland (at times she'd also called herself Jack Beebe and David Bean) in reality was Elvira Virginia Mugarrieta.

She was born in San Francisco, and her father is said to have been the first Mexican consul here and her mother the daughter of a Louisiana Supreme Court justice.

Elvira appears to have masqueraded as a man throughout her adult life.

Her sister claimed she had enlisted in the Army during the Spanish-American War, was honorably discharged with the rank of lieutenant and expressed the hope that the government would give her a funeral with military honors.

More plausible is the tale that she had stowed away aboard a transport heading for the Philippines after war broke out. When discovered, she had to submit to being vaccinated and promptly fainted. Her disguise revealed, she was placed under lock and key.

Then, after reaching Manila, the ship's lights suddenly went out and when, after an hour and a half, they came back on again—Jack Garland had vanished.

Here the plot gets muddy: She either subsequently fought with the troops, served as a "male nurse," or did neither.

At any rate, tattooed on one of her arms were the word "Manila"; the date "1898"; the figures "8" and "29" which supposedly stood for the Eighth Corps Area and the 29th Infantry; a picture of the American flag, and crossed guns.

Returning to San Francisco, she was here during the 1906 Fire and Earthquake and, so the story goes, worked as a Red Cross volunteer with victims of the disaster.

Her last donation—quite possibly her last dollar—had been given to a bewildered, frightened boy who'd run away from home.

She was buried at Cypress Lawn in a plot where other members of her family are interred.

Even in death, Elvira retained an aura of masculinity. For the cemetery records give her correct name plus the notation, "also known as Jack Bee Garland."

Dispensing a Justice

THE STORY has often been told of how Stephen J. Field, associate justice of the U. S. Supreme Court, was attacked in the '80s by David S. Terry in a railroad station restaurant in the town of Lathrop. The latter was shot dead on the spot by the former's bodyguard.

This was an aftermath of one of San Francisco's juiciest trials. Justice Field had presided over the case when Sarah Althea Hill tried to establish that she had been married to William Sharon and, therefore, was entitled to a big chunk of his fortune.

Field had ruled against the lady. (Right or wrong, he *did* have the reputation of siding with the rich against the common herd.) Furthermore, for an erratic outbreak he'd sentenced her and Terry, one of her lawyers, to jail for contempt of court.

Subsequently, Sarah and firebrand Terry who many years earlier had killed David Broderick in that celebrated duel near Lake Merced, were married. Terry had sworn to get Field.

The dramatic incident at Lathrop was the second time Field had escaped possible annihilation at the hands of a Californian.

An "infernal machine" was to have done the job the first time.

In 1864, Field had decided in favor of San Francisco in the complicated "Pueblo" business, which involved titles to property in the city, thereby dispossessing a large number of people who had occupied land as squatters. He'd made a lot of enemies, including one, it would seem, who wanted him wiped out.

Field's long-time connection with California began in December, 1849, when he arrived in Marysville, then a bustling mining town, and was elected mayor three days later.

The son of David Dudley Field, a nationally renowned Congregational clergyman, the dynamic Stephen previously had been practicing law in New York with his brother, David Dudley, Jr.

The following year he was elected to the State Legislature, where he introduced an assortment of bills, laws and regulations.

In 1857 he was elected to the State Supreme Court and two years later, Chief Justice succeeding David S. Terry.

President Lincoln appointed Field to the Nation's Supreme Court in 1863, and he held that post for 34 years, retiring only because of age. In 1869, he also taught law at the University of California.

But all this never would have come to pass if he had opened a little paper-wrapped package delivered to his office in Washington, D.C., in the mid '60s. About four inches square and 1½ inches thick, the parcel bore a San Francisco postmark. At first, for some reason he thought it was a photograph. Then, slitting the paper about one-eighth of an inch he noticed it was a box, became wary and asked a friend present what he should do.

The friend volunteered the opinion that it might be a "torpedo" and suggested dunking it in water.

That done, the two men went into the carriageway under

the Senate steps and shielding themselves behind one of the columns smashed the box against the wall. The lid shattered, exposing the contents.

Sure enough, inside was an ingenious contraption. It was composed of half a dozen copper cartridges, partly filed through, radiating from a cavity filled with powder, and affixed with a "friction match."

If Field had opened the box, there would have been a tremendous explosion and he and his career would have ended with a big boom.

A *Mysterious Kidnaping*

J AMES A. CAMPBELL had been a 20-year-old apprentice seaman when he arrived in the Sandwich Islands in 1850 with only $4 in his jeans and a thick brogue on his tongue.

As this story starts 45 years later, his empire included hundreds of square miles of sugar plantations and cattle ranges, a few blocks of business property in downtown Honolulu, a palatial residence, and heaven knows what all.

The tycoon was as well known in San Francisco's financial and social circles, too, as he was in Hawaii.

He had married a member of a native royal family and the couple produced a quartet of daughters, the two eldest of whom had just been placed in a San Jose school.

The stay of the pair and the younger daughters at San Francisco's Occidental Hotel was just about concluded and they had reservations on a ship sailing for home at nine o'clock on the morning of Tuesday, August 4, 1896.

On the previous afternoon the tall, spare, gray-thatched Scot left the hotel with a middle-aged man wearing a cutaway coat, and together they boarded a Clay street cable car.

When her husband didn't return for dinner Mrs. Campbell

57

wasn't unduly concerned, figuring he probably was hoisting a bon voyage highball or two with cronies.

But she became increasingly alarmed as the night wore on into morning and no word came, although she hesitated to tell anyone of her fears.

Adding to her worry was the knowledge that he had about $350 in cash on him, plus a letter of credit amounting to $10,000.

The news of Campbell's disappearance began to leak out early the next day after bellhops who came for the luggage had been told by his obviously distraught wife that their plans were changed.

Campbell didn't show Tuesday night either.

The town began to tingle.

Then shortly after 9:30 that same evening a haggard and disheveled Campbell, his clothes torn, his face scratched, his head bloody but unbowed, walked unsteadily into the Occidental's lobby, wobbled to the elevator and took it directly to his suite.

Within 20 minutes he was joined behind locked doors by the city's top police captain and a detective to whom he told his story.

The capitalist had left the Occidental Hotel, where he'd been staying with his wife and daughters, accompanied by a man later identified as Oliver Winfield Winthrop.

The ingratiating Winthrop had scraped up an acquaintance with him, Campbell said, on the pretext that he wanted to invest $70,000 in Hawaiian real estate, but his wife was ill and hesitated to make the long voyage.

Would Mr. Campbell please try to persuade her to go?

Campbell first fluffed him off but eventually agreed, and the two men went ostensibly to Winthrop's house 'way out on California street between Third and Fourth avenues.

However, instead of an ailing lady there, a masked man pointed a revolver at Campbell's head and told him to put up his hands. But the elderly, rugged financier made a flying tackle.

In the ensuing melee the gun went off, piercing his hat and creasing his skull. Whereupon Winthrop entered the act and clubbed him into unconsciousness.

When Campbell came to, the pair demanded that he write a check for $20,000 plus a note to his wife instructing her to cash same and turn the money over the bearer or they'd kill him.

Campbell just sneered. He was probably not long for this world anyhow he said and he invited them to murder away.

So he was handcuffed, chained to a bed and threatened with torture. He refused all proffered food and drink for fear of being poisoned and lay seething.

Winthrop wandered in and out, leaving his masked partner, Pete, in charge, and their defiant victim continued to tell them to go to the devil.

Nevertheless, he was growing weak from hunger and loss of blood.

Then, some time on Wednesday, Winthrop, dapper and jovial, breezed in and announced that he was off on a brief pleasure trip to Mexico.

He told Pete that if Campbell hadn't capitulated by the next day to release him, and had the gall to give the old man some fatherly advice about not trusting strangers.

Pete tried one more piece of strategy: He removed Campbell's shoes and socks, lighted a cigar and made as if to burn his feet.

When Campbell merely muttered, "Go ahead," Pete apparently lost heart and decided to chuck the whole business then and there.

So he unchained Campbell, returned all his effects except the money, handed him the brand-new hat Winthrop had brought to replace the bullet-scarred one, and turned him loose—with a nickel for carfare.

Some San Franciscans were suspicious of the preposterous-sounding story Campbell related.

Couldn't this yarn about his terrible ordeal at the hands of kidnappers have been a cover-up for 52 hours of fun and frivolity?

But when Oliver Winfield Winthrop was identified as the principal villain in the piece, even the most doubting of Thomases began to give credence to the elderly Scot's tale.

For Winthrop was a weird one. A former assistant superintendent at the Laurel Hill Cemetery, he had starred in a sensational case just the previous year.

Though natty, genial and ingratiating of manner, he had been accused of presenting a mother with a strychnine pill as she sat by the grave of her infant child.

He was tried for murder.

The jury disagreed, though, and he was freed. Just the same . . .

At any rate, a couple of weeks after Campbell's kidnaping, Winthrop, disguised in shapeless clothes, wearing blue goggles and walking with an exaggerated limp, was apprehended in Oakland.

At first he tried to bluff it through, pretending to be someone else. Then he began to enjoy the limelight.

When the trial started he would nod and exchange pleasantries with acquaintances in the courtroom, hum snatches of popular tunes and bite huge chunks of the plug tobacco he always carried in his pocket.

The prosecution paraded in a series of witnesses with damaging and conclusive evidence, especially one Donald Archibald Urquhart.

He testified that Winthrop had suggested they organize a sort of kidnaping company for the purpose of holding wealthy people for ransom and even had nominated Campbell as a good subject to start the business.

Urbane and presumably unruffled, Winthrop took the stand and insisted that this was all nonsense.

Actually, he explained patiently, Urquhart had approached *him* with an offer of $50 if he'd rent a cottage and later bring out Campbell who was known to like a bit of fun.

Meanwhile Urquhart, according to Winthrop, would stock the house with booze and a couple of agreeable dollies.

Although the whole immoral idea revolted him, Winthrop managed to stifle his scruples and fell in with the plan.

So on Monday afternoon August 3, he escorted Campbell to the place of assignation and was told to come back at dusk and fetch him.

But when he returned no one answered the bell, nor was he any more successful on several subsequent attempts.

That the house still was occupied he could tell by the sounds of revelry—laughter and the tinkle of glasses.

Finally, disgusted with the sordid situation, he left for good. And that, beamed the bland Winthrop, was all he knew.

The jurors weren't impressed. It took them exactly five minutes to bring in a guilty verdict.

Winthrop was sentenced to life imprisonment, paroled from San Quentin 17 years later, sent to prison again in May 1926 and died the following month in Folsom.

Ghastly Murders in a Church

THE CENTRAL figures in one of San Francisco's most grisly murder cases were: (1) Theodore Durrant, a Cooper College Medical student and Sunday School superintendent at the Emmanuel Baptist Church on Bartlett Street; (2) Blanche Lamont, a gentle, innocent student at Girls' Normal School; and (3) Minnie Williams, a somewhat cynical sophisticated miss from a broken family.

Both girls, also active in the church, had been friends of the dapper Durrant, although Blanche was believed to have been his fiancee.

On April 3, 1895, Blanche disappeared, generating a tremendous commotion. She had been last seen in the company of Durrant, but as he was considered a model youth no shadow of suspicion descended on him at the time.

On Good Friday, April 12, Minnie, who had been noticed entering the church with him that evening, also vanished, causing somewhat less consternation.

The following day a contingent of flower-laden ladies bent upon decorating the church for Easter, found Minnie's stabbed, mutilated and molested body in the library's closet.

Police searching the building the next morning came upon

the remains of Blanche in the belfry. Nude, her head rested on a block of wood, her hands folded across her chest. She'd been strangled but not assaulted.

That afternoon Durrant was apprehended near Walnut Creek and arrested for Blanche's murder. The news swept through the town like a grass fire and hordes of furious citizens awaited his arrival at the Ferry Building, many pursuing up Market street the hack that transported him to jail.

It took six weeks to question 1400 veniremen before a jury could be impaneled. Crowds, mostly women, fought to get into the courtroom when the trial opened on September 3.

Though protesting his innocence, which he did until the very end, Durrant consistently kept his cool as a chain of circumstantial evidence tightened around him.

Perhaps the most damaging bit of testimony was that offered by a pawnbroker who maintained that Durrant, without success, had tried to hock Blanche's rings, which later were sent anonymously to her aunt, with whom she'd lived.

The city seethed and rocked with rumors during the two-month trial.

Then, on November 1, the jury deliberated only 28 minutes before bringing in a guilty verdict. But due to a series of appeals that ultimately extended to the U. S. Supreme Court, the sentence wasn't carried out until January 7, 1898, when he was hanged at San Quentin.

(Durrant never was tried for the murder of Minnie, who conceivably was killed because she had learned of Blanche's demise.)

Even then, the ghastly business wasn't over. No funeral director in town would accept Durrant's body for cremation, and a story goes that his parents took it to their Mission District home while they sought one who would.

Finally an agreeable undertaker was located in Pasadena. Angry mobs waiting for the train at the station in Los Angeles were foiled when the coffin was removed at Glendale.

A Family's Eccentric End

M T. DAVIDSON, San Francisco's highest hill and site of the annual Sunrise Service, is a monument to Professor George Davidson.

Once part of the San Miguel Rancho and later a portion of 12,000 acres owned by Adolph Sutro, the peak was known as Blue Mountain when Davidson surveyed it in 1862.

But by the time it was dedicated a public park in 1929, on the 83rd birthday of John McLaren, it already had been called by the name of the distinguished Davidson for many years.

Incidentally, he also has a mountain in Nevada and an island off Alaska named for him.

A native of Nottingham, England, he had come to this country when he was seven years old, and with his parents settled in Philadelphia. Davidson's genius presumably became apparent early, for at 17 he was given a responsible position in the observatory at Girard's College.

Eight years later he headed an expedition to the West for a U.S. Survey. Thereafter, except for extensive travel, he made San Francisco his home.

During his long, fruitful life, Davidson published more than 3000 books, treatises and reports, covering a wide and diversified range of scientific subjects.

American and European countries bestowed some 35 awards on him. Numerous foreign rulers decorated him, and although his formal education had ended at high school, several universities gave him honorary degrees.

In the early '70s Davidson set up a telescope on Lafayette Square, the first such in the City, and maintained it privately for two decades. Through that instrument his friend James Lick got his first intimate glimpse of heavenly bodies, which were to fascinate him for the remainder of his life, and prompt him to leave $700,000 for the founding of an observatory on Mt. Hamilton.

In 1858 Davidson married Ellinor Fauntleroy of Virginia, a descendant of a noble British family. She was the granddaughter of Robert Owen, a famed and dedicated Welsh philanthropist who founded a number of "ideal" communities, including one in New Harmony, Indiana.

Theirs appears to have been a happy union, lasting to their golden wedding anniversary in 1908 when Ellinor died. Her husband survived her by three years.

It was a different story with the couple's three children, though.

Their younger son, George, committed suicide in 1900 at the age of 30.

After a stark and lonely life his brother Thomas died suddenly in 1934. Ellinor, their only daughter, developed into an eccentric.

For over 10 years following the death of Thomas, Ellinor Davidson lived alone in the four-story family house at 2221 Washington street.

Thomas is said to have been an inventor of sorts, claiming to have dreamed up the stop-and-go traffic signal, and he liked

to tinker with the innards of watches. But he had his pecu-
liarities.

An expert researcher in a prominent local law firm, he chose
4 p.m. to midnight as his working hours. Although crime was
at considerably lower ebb in those days, he apparently feared
being held up. So it was his custom to seal his valuables in
a self-addressed, stamped envelope before leaving the office,
presumably in order to stuff it in a mailbox should a thief
attack.

On the final night of his life, he arrived home, placed his
hat on the downstairs hall table, went up to his room and
died of a heart attack.

A decade later, the police, alerted by disturbed neighbors
who had seen no activity in the house for several days, broke
in. The hat was still in the same place. They found Ellinor
dead in bed.

They found a myriad of other things in the dismal dwelling,
too — much junk, but also a great deal of valuable material.

Although Ellinor had been heir to a $245,000 fortune, elec-
tricity never had been installed in the house. She had used
candles for illumination and their flickering light had invested
the gloomy abode with a particularly eerie aura at night.

For a full year before Ellinor's demise, a representative of
a legal firm that was executor of the Davidson estate had
been organizing and cataloging literally thousands of items.
There were vanloads of priceless books, maps, papers and
scientific instruments that had belonged to her famed father,
as well as souvenirs, relics and objects of art.

A card on a lovely lacquered cabinet, a gift to Davidson
from the Japanese government, indicated that it was to be
shipped to the Metropolitan Museum in New York.

On a wall in one of the three large living rooms hung a
handsome landscape by William Keith; and on another, a mas-
sive moose head. Stuffed owls sat on the floor in an upstairs

hall, and an American flag with 35 stars was draped over Davidson's bedstead.

Workmen prying open the door of one closet gasped as they came upon a grisly sight — a dozen human skulls. These proved to be anthropological specimens that Davidson had brought back from an expedition to the South Pacific.

When the men ripped open the door to the closet in the professor's study, they discovered five urns. The vases contained the ashes of Ellinor's mother, father, two brothers and an aunt.

III

Rags to Riches

He Was Afraid of Nothing—Except Horses

MUCH OF the credit for rebuilding San Francisco both in the downtown and residential areas after the Fire and Earthquake must go to Willis Polk who died in 1924 at the comparatively early age of 56.

The impressive and astonishing list of his structures—over 100 from 1906 to 1914 alone—includes office buildings, banks, garages, churches, clubs, water and power stations and railroad terminals as well as mansions. The astounding breadth of his talent is realized when such diversified examples of his work are considered as the Spreckels, Hobart and Mills Buildings, St. Mary's Hospital, and the Spring Valley Water Pumping Station.

Out-of-the-city designs include Filoli, the Woodside estate built for the William B. Bourns; St. Matthew's Catholic Church in San Mateo, and the exquisite water temple at Sunol, which it is said he considered his masterpiece.

Debonair, dapper and witty, Polk confused and confounded those who erroneously thought him too much of the erratic artist to be a practical architect. He didn't cotton much to the word "architect" anyway, preferring to refer to himself as a master builder.

Rather dandified in appearance, he had small feet, sensitive hands and a domeshaped head.

But he had the courage of his convictions and the fortitude to express them freely and fiercely—a fact that often catapulted him into the caldrons of burning dissension and argument.

Although Polk did more than any other man to mold this city into the metropolis it is today, he wasn't a native son. He was born in Kentucky while his father (who also was an architect as well as his father before him) was fighting in the Civil War as a colonel with the Confederate Army. The family was well off, lived on a plantation and owned 18 slaves.

Then came catastrophe. Polk's father returned from the war an almost helpless cripple at 25 and found himself financially destitute. The Polks moved to St. Louis, where the mother, a gently reared Southern woman, took in washing and boarders.

Willis, then six, helped out by selling newspapers on the street, later augmenting his income by working for a hatter and hardware merchant. In the summer with what time was left over he sold lemonade, made by his mother, at five cents a glass. He never went to school but garnered what learning he could from his father.

One day he saw an advertisement in a paper asking for plans for a schoolhouse to be built in Hope, Arkansas. He whipped some out, sent them in and won the contract. When he appeared to direct the work they thought the winner had sent his son. Willis was just 15.

Puckish Polk is the hero of innumerable yarns. For instance:

When the Hobart Building, one of a great many which he designed, was under construction, the Board of Supervisors sent a building inspector to stop the progress. The method of fire-proofing the floor beams didn't conform to regulations, they maintained. Polk puffed calmly on a cigar and told the official that as the foreman now on the tenth floor was engaged in that work he had better tell him.

So the poor harassed inspector climbed laboriously and precariously to the assigned floor of the skeleton building only to be informed by the foreman that he wouldn't quit unless Polk told him to. Down the inspector trudged, to find that an enchanted crowd had gathered to see the fun.

"Are you going to stop or aren't you?" thundered the inspecter to the serene Polk.

"Get a policeman and make me," snapped the architect. "That ordinance was framed by a bunch of incompetents. As the so-called crime is being committed on the tenth floor, you'll have to go up there to get me."

With that he boarded a steel girder, signaled to the man at the donkey engine and soared aloft. But the inspector had had enough of climbing. Apparently he couldn't entice any cop to get airborne either, for when Polk returned to terra firma there was no one present to carry on the argument.

Polk was a member of such august organizations as the Pacific Union, Bohemian and Burlingame Country Clubs. He also was a full-fledged member of the Stonecutters' Union. What's more, he had proved his worth to get into the latter by demonstrating his skill with mallet, chisel and square. As an active card-bearing unionist he was required to march in the Labor Day parade. This he was ready and eager to do.

The Brothers, proud of their illustrious member, promptly elected him marshal for the day. That meant he was expected to lead them, wearing a sash and riding a prancing steed. Polk didn't shy at the sash, but he did at the horse. His chums in the more fashionable tongs, hearing of his appointment, delightedly sent him cushions and bandages and arnica.

"My seat fits a club chair better than a saddle," Polk muttered as he hurriedly left for Chicago on a sudden business call.

Tale Of A Bitter Tycoon

THE 110-year-old James Lick house in the Santa Clara Valley is a memorial to a romance that went sour.

But Lick never lived in that pleasant, two-storied, porticoed residence. Indeed, he didn't even finish it. He had built it to keep his illegitimate son with him. John, though, didn't want it or his father, either.

James Lick, generally conceded to be one of California's greatest benefactors, occupied a shanty nearby, and there slept on a cot contrived of a door set on four empty nail kegs.

When in San Francisco he lived in a dreary back room of the Lick House, his lavish and luxurious hotel at Montgomery and Sutter streets.

He'd constructed on the property near San Jose, however, a magnificent flour mill—a defiant monument to a galling incident that changed the course of his life.

Lick and the daughter of a prosperous miller fell in love during his young manhood in Pennsylvania. When the girl announced that she was pregnant, Lick asked her father for her hand.

The irate miller refused, sneering at Lick's poverty and

pointing out what a fine establishment *he* had. Lick left this unhappy interview vowing that someday he'd own a mill finer than the old man's.

An expert cabinetmaker, Lick specialized in piano cases, and he soon left for South America to ply his trade. He stayed a dozen years and ran up a modest fortune of about $40,000.

He must have assumed that time stood still in Pennsylvania. For upon returning, he hired the fanciest horse and buggy he could find and went to dazzle the lady-love who had borne him a son.

But the miller's daughter had married. She wanted no part of Lick.

So he returned to South America and finally, an embittered man in his early 50's, arrived in San Francisco in January, 1848, and began to buy real estate.

He acquired about 40 parcels in all—one lot, at what became Powell and Sutter, cost $16, for instance, and he paid $150 for a large piece at Fourth and Market.

Then came the Gold Rush. Land values zoomed, and Lick's investments burgeoned to such a degree that he became the richest man in town.

He also had bought many acres near San Jose, and it was there that he decided to build the mill that would surpass that of the man who had sneered at him.

It was three stories high: two of brick, the top of perfect redwood timbers. Inside, it was fitted with carved and polished beams of Spanish cedar and mahogany and the newest and costliest machinery.

When the mill was finished he had a photographer shoot it from all angles and sent the packet of pictures to his old antagonist in the East.

But despite his crusty and dour disposition, Lick had grown to love his Santa Clara Valley property and planted acres of fruit orchards and breathtaking gardens.

People snickered when the gruff, unfriendly man in greasy clothes drove a rickety wagon about begging for bones. But he ground those bones into fertilizer and his trees and plants flourished.

Lick was pushing 60 when, for some reason, his illegitimate son, John, came West to visit him. Understandably, perhaps, the long-awaited meeting was not a success.

A feckless young man, John frittered away his days doing odd jobs or reading novels and wouldn't even stir enough to enjoy the extravagances his usually penurious father urged on him. They managed to irritate each other prodigiously.

At last John accepted a year of travel in Europe, but when he returned to California it was the same old thing. Himself content to live in hovels or dismal hotel rooms, Lick thought he might persuade his son to remain with him if he built them an attractive house.

But before the place was completed, John returned to the East, an act that was to cost him most of his father's estate.

So at 75 Lick was alone again. He had plenty of company five years later, however, when he lay dying in the Lick House.

Besides the doctors and nurses in attendance, trustees of his estate, members of the California Pioneer Society (of which he was president) and reporters were permitted to trot in and out of his chilly, shabby room until he breathed his last.

Fortunately for San Francisco, Lick was fully aware of his reputation as an eccentric. So when he knew death was near he took the precaution of having a panel of medics examine him to prove that he was of sound mind.

He willed son John $150,000 in gold coin (he got a bit more later) and earmarked most of the remainder of his $4 million fortune for public benefactions.

A few months after his burial, Lick's body was disinterred from the Masonic Cemetery and taken to Mount Hamilton.

There his coffin was lowered into the foundation pier of the great telescope that became his heavenly headstone.

He Was King Of A Vast Empire

WHAT MANNER of man was cattle king Henry Miller, founder of the Miller and Lux fortune?

He left $40 million—80 per cent of which was eventually divvied up among eight descendants after undoubtedly the longest, most complex and bitter legal battle ever witnessed in San Francisco or possibly anywhere else.

In the first place, his name wasn't "Miller" at all.

Moreover, it's possible he never would have come to California if a casual friend hadn't fallen in love.

Miller was born Heinrich Alfred Kreiser in 1827 in Backenheim, a small German hamlet.

He began to earn his own living at eight, and by the time he was 12 showed signs of the business acumen that eventually made him the mogul of a Western U.S. empire twice the size of Belgium.

For he bought sheep and cattle at bargain prices and drove them to his father's butcher shop and packing house.

But Heinrich had set his sights on a far wider horizon. While still in his teens he went to Holland, then England and finally to New York, arriving in 1847, and there served as a butcher's apprentice for a couple of years.

Meanwhile he had made the acquaintance of Henry Miller, a young shoe clerk who, wanting to get in on the Gold Rush, had booked passage for San Francisco.

However, when sailing time approached Miller couldn't bear to tear himself away from his sweetheart.

So Heinrich bought his ticket and took his name as well.

He got here in 1850 via the Isthmus of Panama, with $6 in his jeans, and found a job with a French butcher.

But working for someone else wasn't Henry's way. The following year he leased a lot on Jackson street, erected a one-story building and struck out on his own.

Miller proceeded to invest his earnings in hogs and in producing superior pork sausages, which he peddled. In 1853 he racked up a record by delivering the first herd of cattle ever driven to San Francisco.

His partnership with Charles Lux, another German, was formed in 1858. It was a dual relationship, by the way, as the men married sisters.

Presumably Lux furnished most of the capital, while Miller brought to the alliance, which subsequently became internationally known, tremendous energy, colossal shrewdness, ruthless, stubborn drive and, as someone had said, "a morbid dread of being outwitted or overreached."

But most of all his credo was to buy land and *keep* it.

"Only fools sell," he often said.

He preferred to ride the range, keeping close personal tab on every acre and each man employed on his vast properties, which covered not only California but chunks of Oregon and Nevada as well.

Waste and negligence offended his very soul and the story goes that he would tip over garbage cans to see what and how much was being thrown away.

Miller also was a stickler for discipline and detail.

After laying down the law to a foreman or other hired hand

(he imported a crew of relatives from the old country to work for him) he'd follow the lecture with several pages of instructions, suggestions and solid thought.

Some of these homilies have been preserved. For example:

"I can stand severe losses where unavoidable but losses due to carelessness and inattention are unbearable.

"Unbranded calves . . . is [sic] bad business as it might induce some of our neighbors to be dishonest.

"A good employee is one that goes out of his way to make a saving and profit for his employer.

"No man with backbone is willing to do a woman's work on a farm."

And perhaps the most significant of all:

"There is a class of people not made to be prosperous."

At the crest of their wave in 1887, Lux suddenly died.

At Miller's suggestion the partners had made a pact stipulating that in the event of either's death the survivor would carry on the business for at least seven years.

Shortly thereafter began a shuffling and complicated maneuvering that despite the materialization of 27 Lux "heirs" culminated in 1910 with Miller gaining sole control and possession of the entire empire.

In June, following the 1906 fire, Miller, whose Rincon Hill house and everything in it had been destroyed, bought the elegant mansion of Horace L. Hill on the northwest corner of Sacramento and Laguna streets.

The deal was the largest and most important residential sale to take place since the holocaust. It was in that dwelling that the once vigorous Miller, then pushing 90 and a widower since 1905, died a decade later.

The Man Who Owned The City

ADOLPH SUTRO was next to the oldest of the 13 children brought to the U.S. from Germany by his widowed mother, who settled her brood in Maryland. But California's gold rush called him west and he arrived in San Francisco in 1850.

However, it was through silver, not gold, that Adolph was destined to make his fortune.

As a small-time merchant dealing principally in cigars and tobacco, Sutro remained in this vicinity for nine years.

He hit for Nevada in 1859 and there quickly realized that the mining methods used at Virginia City's Comstock Lode were outmoded, inadequate and needlessly expensive. Moreover, they were dangerous.

So with a little knowledge of mineralogy picked up in the Old Country, he advocated building a tunnel that would lower the brutal heat in the mines and drain off the great volumes of water that constantly flooded the deeper shafts.

At first the idea was thought entirely nutty. Later, though, when it not only appeared sound but gave every indication of reaping rich royalties, the men who dominated the Comstock wanted it for their own.

So they started a titanic fight to the finish on all fronts.

Nevertheless, the aggressive immigrant, a hurricane of energy and a persuasive speaker despite his fractured English, proved to be equally as rough and tough as the Big Boys.

He finally managed to finance his venture with Eastern and European capital and completed the project in 1878.

Not long afterward he sold out, pocketed millions and returned to San Francisco.

Sutro began to buy thousands of what were generally considered worthless acres.

Eventually, his staggering real estate empire extended from Bakers Beach and Lincoln Park to the shores of Lake Merced.

In between were such vast areas as most of the present Richmond and Sunset districts, West Portal, Forest Hill, St. Francis Wood and Westwood Park, as well as all of Sutro Forest, which included one of the highest points in the city and was formerly part of the old San Miguel Rancho.

Then, of course there were The Heights, commanding a miles-long vista of the Pacific shoreline.

Sutro and his daughter Emma used to ride their horses out to the windswept promontory. He fell in love with it and decided to make his home there and spent a million or so improving the property. He constructed a stable and stocked it with thoroughbreds.

He laid out extensive formal gardens boasting terraces, lawns, grottos and arbors, imported a profusion of exotic plants, shrubs and trees and studded the grounds with statuary.

Defying papa's fury, Emma became one of the first women medical students at the University of California and served on the staff of Children's Hospital for a couple of decades.

She must have been as fond of The Heights as her father. For after his death in 1898 and during the family's subsequent legal squabbles that took 21 years to settle, she bought out the other heirs' interests and continued to live there.

Although she had previously deeded the estate to the city,

Emma died in the old home in 1938 at the age of 82. The house was demolished the following year.

Sutro Heights at night, especially when the fog creeps in from the Pacific and shrouds the old trees or when the raw, salt-laden winds sear the cheek and rattle dead branches, can be as cheerless as Wuthering Heights.

But when the weather is balmy and the evenings mild, this elevation can take on a pleasantly eerie enchantment and become suitable for a setting of a production of "A Midsummer Night's Dream."

It was under the latter circumstances, undoubtedly, that some years ago a local dancer named Beatrice Lewis had envisioned it when she conceived a ballet called "A Night in Sutro Gardens."

After she produced her Sutro opus late in 1939, she gained much favorable notice and her career took a decided spurt.

Arrangements were being made to present the ballet again at the Golden Gate International Exposition on Treasure Island when, for reasons known only to herself, she went out to The Heights one March day in 1940.

A witness later recalled seeing the dancer seated on the stone parapet where during the days of Adolph Sutro's residency, tall classic statues had alternated with urns.

Glancing in the same direction a bit later, this same person was horrified to see the ballerina's body hurtle down the steep 250-foot cliff and land with a sickening crash on the concrete pavement below.

Beatrice Lewis died in an ambulance on the way to the hospital.

Police who found her briefcase half way down the descent decided that she had slipped—possibly on the juicy ice plant that grew on the slope—and listed her death as accidental.

But there still are those superstitious few who shun The Heights for fear of being pushed to their doom by some dark, unknown force.

The Man They Called Lucky

THE DEATH of Dextra Baldwin McGonagle in Arcadia in February, 1967, passed unnoticed in San Francisco and, as far as we know, there was no mention in the local press of her funeral there four days later.

Mrs. McGonagle was cremated and her ashes placed in the mausoleum at Cypress Lawn which also contains the remains of her mother, Anita Baldwin, and her grandfather Elias Jackson "Lucky" Baldwin as well as several other relatives.

The Baldwin name may not mean much around San Francisco today. The clan has made its headquarters in Southern California for many years, and "E. J.," the family's founder, owned the vast Santa Anita Ranch, site of the famed race track. He spent his last decade or so on the ranch, and died there in 1909.

But at one time the Baldwin name was big in Northern California.

The story, of course, begins with the robust "Lucky," a nick name, it's said, that annoyed him. He liked to think that he'd acquired everything through his own endeavors and not a favorable fate.

However there's many a tale to the contrary, be it fact or fiction.

Born in Ohio in 1828, Lucky Baldwin tried his hand at a number of diverse jobs — farming, storekeeping, hotel running and horsetrading — before coming to California, where a talent for the last two occupations especially was to stand him in good stead.

Baldwin may not have considered himself lucky. Nevertheless he usually managed to make the scene just as things were beginning to move fast.

For instance he arrived in California four years after the Gold Rush, just in time to hit the building boom, and later pulled a fortune out of the Comstock when the Virginia City silver mines already were producing millions.

Heading a small party, he had set out across the plains in March, 1853, with four wagonloads of merchandise which he sold at a solid profit in Salt Lake City. The group arrived in Placerville that August but Baldwin wasted little time there, came to San Francisco, and invested in real estate. Land brought good prices which he invested in more land.

Although he knew nothing about bricks, he purchased half an interest in a brickyard and wangled a lucrative U.S. government contract to construct buildings at Fort Mason and on Alcatraz island.

And he had a passion for hotels exceeded only by that for women and horses — a nice parlay.

Baldwin owned and operated a succession of small hotels around town. But his crowning achievement in that field was his $3-million Baldwin Hotel erected in the late '70s on the corner of Powell and Market. The six-story "skyscraper," voted the finest in the West in its day, contained a handsome theater.

He built hotels at Lake Tahoe where he owned much acreage, in Arcadia and in the mountains outside of Los Angeles, too.

He really hit the Big Time on the Comstock and for a while

shared billing with such other flamboyant Comstock kings as Fair, Flood, Mackay, and Ralston.

Just the same he had been financially pressed when calamity stuck in 1898 and the Baldwin Hotel burned to the ground. Five people lost their lives in the holocaust and Baldwin lost his shirt. He didn't have a cent of insurance.

This disaster marked a geographical turning point in his life. Baldwin sold the property to James L. Flood for a million or so and, not long after, left for Santa Anita to raise race horses. This he did with equal eclat and soon his horses were as well known in Saratoga and Lexington as in California.

His personal life was something else. Judging from the be-whiskered pictures we've seen it's hard to think of him as a Lothario but such certainly seems to have been the case. In addition to four marriages he presumably had any given number of extracurricular adventures. All sorts of ladies and alleged offspring turned up after his death demanding pieces of his estate.

He left some $11 million, mostly divided between his daughters, Clara and Anita. Anita stayed on to run the ranch and stables.

The widow Baldwin and another daughter—who was not known to have been his until after he died—got comparatively short shrift. Mrs. Baldwin sued and eventually won a better settlement.

He Never Quite Made It

DAVID D. COLTON, whose name has gone down in the same historical chapters that deal with the railroad-building Big Four — albeit slightly behind — began his career in California as a sheriff.

When in the spring of 1850 gold was discovered in the Mt. Shasta region, Colton, then visiting in Portland, headed for Siskiyou county and was elected to the sheriff's post there at the age of 21.

Futhermore, through a series of exploits in local skirmishes, he won the regard of Governor Bigler, who showed his appreciation rather expansively by appointing him a brigadier general in the state militia.

Thereafter and forevermore Dave affected a military bearing and enjoyed using the title, although he never saw any army duty — peaceful or hostile.

He'd left his father's house in Maine to seek fame and fortune in the West, and in less than a quarter of a century he found both.

But eventually his reputation became somewhat clouded

and, outsmarted by conniving associates, he had a comparatively small estate to pass on when he died.

Red-haired, stocky and cocky, with a driving ambition and
no overabundance of scruples, he came well-equipped to hold
his own in the rugged wrestling on the frontier.

Although shrewd and wily, he nevertheless could be taken
in on occasion — as will be seen.

Not one to stay in the backwoods, Colton came to San Francisco in short order and developed what must have been a
close friendship with Senator David C. Broderick. He was one
of the latter's seconds at that famed duel on the shores of
Lake Merced in 1859 when Broderick was fatally punctured
by still another David — Judge Terry.

After Broderick's death, Colton helped to keep his political
organization together for a while. He also acquired some
chunks of the deceased's real estate holdings, which subsequently became valuable. His period of prosperity appears
to date from this point.

After the Civil War, Colton went East and studied law —
a process that didn't take long in those days — then returned
and went into practice with a former classmate.

But Dave wasn't one to sit in an office and wait for clients.
He set about ingratiating himself with acquaintances in high
places.

He got caught in the web of one flamboyant flop, though.
This was the great diamond hoax of 1871 in which many another hot-shot (including his friend, banker William C. Ralston) also was hooked.

Accustomed as they were to seeing vast fortunes made virtually overnight, Californians were ripe for the get-rich-quick
scheme by a couple of slick con men posing as poor-but-honest
prospectors.

If the plot was elaborate, the reward was well worth the

time and trouble involved. A group of the canniest characters on the coast were taken in by tales of a fantastically loaded diamond mine in Colorado and formed a $10-million company to handle it. The "discoverers" were content with $600,000 for their share.

Colton was made manager. But before he had time to complete furnishing his fancy office, the swindle was exposed and the prospectors had taken a powder.

Oh, the diamonds were there all right. The field had been salted — strewn in conspicuous places with low grade sparklers bought secretly in Europe. Some had even been cut.

As a snickering nation enjoyed the joke, the corporation was dissolved and Colton went on to edge into the aura of the Big Four.

Colton was a sort of fifth wheel on the Big Four wagon composed of Crocker, Stanford, Hopkins and Huntington.

Wise in the ways of manipulating politicos, he pulled wires, greased palms, performed unpleasant tasks and assorted skullduggery for the railroad magnates and served as their financial director for a time.

However, this aggressive, red-headed New Englander was never quite "one of the boys." (He was also occasionally called the fraction of the Big 4 1/2!)

Charles Crocker appeared to be his friend — with reservations. Leland Stanford tended to snub him. Collis P. Huntington tolerated him because he was useful and hard-working, while dour Mark Hopkins heartily disliked and mistrusted him and made no bones about it.

Nevertheless, Colton's association with the impressive quartet, plus his own acumen, placed him in the limelight, if not exactly in a rosy glow.

Moreover, his wife began to figure conspicuously in local society and his two pretty daughters were popular. Their entertainments, travels and house parties at the Coltons' country place near Mount Diablo were duly recorded in the social columns of the era.

The family occupied the handsomest mansion on Nob Hill, which, after Colton died, was bought by Huntington. The site was given to the city by Mrs. Huntington in 1915, and now is the little park bearing that name.

Although made of wood painted white, the house was believed to have been a copy of a marble villa in Italy, and unlike the tortured, turreted monstrosities of his colleagues and neighbors, was simple and classic in design.

It was in this house that Colton died.

Around 10 o'clock on the night of October 8, 1878, he was carried from a carriage past the crouched lions on the steps and into his residence.

Soon after, two of the town's best-known doctors arrived. They were followed by several other men, including his secretary and law partner.

His wife and younger daughter — the other girl had married — were in New York.

The lights in the house remained on all night, while stories swept through the city that Colton had been murdered — specifically, stabbed.

This was given credence, due to the fact that there were many who hated his innards and he previously had been threatened in posters tacked to buildings and poles in the financial district.

But reporters were told that, some days earlier, the horse he had been riding at his Diablo estate had thrown him — despite the fact that he was known to have been an excellent rider.

Although the injuries he sustained were not believed to have been serious at the time, he had been ruptured. An internal abscess had formed and blood poisoning developed.

Colton died at 47 two days later.

A *Tough Tycoon's Soft Spot*

THOMAS H. BLYTHE was a cold, cynical and aloof man. Yet he had moments of tenderness.

The black suit and high hat he usually wore enhanced his forbidding demeanor and he seemed to have no friends, unless one counted the four large dogs always at his side.

Born Thomas Williams in Wales in 1822, he worked briefly in drapers' and clothing shops as a youth before starting a contracting firm of his own. When that failed, he changed his name and course of life and sailed for California, arriving in San Francisco in the wake of the first Forty-Niners.

Within a few years he made a shrewd move. By means of a mortgage foreclosure, he acquired the triangular block bounded by Market, Grant avenue and Geary for $1100. He took over the adjoining block edged by Stockton and O'Farrell soon after for another paltry sum. Then he had merely to wait and watch the city grow . . . and his fortune with it.

In 1873, Blythe visited England and there had a fling with one Miss Julia Perry, who in due course bore him a daughter, Florence. But by this time Tom was back in California.

He developed a deep devotion in absentia for the child. In addition to sending her a small monthly stipend, he wrote her lengthy letters laying plans for the day when she would be old enough to join him here. He even built a house on Russian Hill for her. (It would appear, however, that he exhibited no great concern for the welfare of Mother Julia).

In the interim, Blythe put machinery into motion to carry out what was then thought to be a fantastic idea. This was to transform the arid desert in the extreme Southeastern portion of the State into a lush, fertile valley by irrigating it with water from the Colorado River.

To this end he filed claim on 40,000 acres along the river under the Swamp and Overflow Act and engaged engineers to blast a canal bed through solid granite.

The project was nearing completion in November, 1882, when Blythe viewed it for the last time. Less than six months later — on April 4, 1883 — he died of a paralytic stroke in his rooms above a Geary street saloon and the imaginative undertaking came to an abrupt halt. The little Southern California town of Blythe serves as his memorial.

Poor Tom was placed in a metal coffin which remained in a mortuary for a year while contestants, singly and in groups, materialized from all over to lay claim to shares in the $4-million estate he'd left to Florence.

The legal struggle, one of the fiercest fought and most sensational and highly publicized in California history, went on for nearly a quarter of a century. Meanwhile, many of the ramshackle buildings Blythe had erected in the 1850s remained on the choice city property until they were swept away in the 1906 Fire.

The litigation finally ended the following year, with Florence given title to her father's extensive holdings. She became a notable social figure and renowned hostess in the Bay Area, as well as in New York and Paris, and was married and widowed three times.

Her first husband, Fritz Hinckley, was an Oakland capitalist. When he died, she married A. A. Moore, Jr., a prominent local attorney who'd been one of her lawyers in the prolonged lawsuit. He was killed in an accident.

Dr. William Everett Musgrave of San Francisco, a nationally recognized physician, public health expert and author, her third spouse, died in 1927.

The daughter Tom Blythe had never seen but so generously provided for died in Oakland in February, 1941.

From Dreams To Despair

A GRAY GRANITE monument that looks as if it started out to be a fountain stands isolated on the Marina Green.

Bronze fishes with wide-open mouths from which, it's presumed, water was designed to flow into basins beneath are on two sides of the thick rectangular shaft.

A bronze bas-relief bust of William C. Ralston done by the eminent sculptor Haig Patigian is on the flank facing town. Ralston, the pioneer banker who conceived and built the first Palace Hotel, drowned in the Bay after his financial empire crumbled.

Under this are the dates 1826–1875 and the inscription "He blazed the path for San Francisco's onward march to achievement and renown."

Below the heroic metal figure of a woman (also in relief) on the bayward side are the words "Memorial to William Chapman Ralston erected by San Francisco through the generous gift of Major Edward Bowes. 1941."

A lot of people who've stopped while walking their dogs long enough to read the above undoubtedly have been perplexed by it. The younger set, assuming they knew who Ralston was, probably thought the donor to have been some distinguished military figure.

Senior citizens, however, will recognize the major as the rather dour emcee of a once highly popular national network radio amateur hour, but may wonder how *he* got into the act.

Although Bowes was coy about this age, it's generally assumed that he was born in San Francisco, which both loved so dearly, only a year or two after Ralston's death in 1875.

Each man had the ability to amass wealth and the propensity to live it up luxuriously.

Both, in time, lost their riches, but the astute Bowes managed to recoup his and leave an estate upward of $3 million.

He used a small portion of that to erect the monument on the Marina Green.

Bowes' father was a weigher on the local waterfront when he died leaving his widow with three small children.

The oldest, 6 year-old Edward, attended Lincoln Grammar School, where he learned to pen a flowery Spencerian script.

The skill came in handy and he earned money by copying legal papers and writing ladies' calling cards for 25 cents a dozen.

At 13 he was working as an office boy in a real estate firm. He soon owned the outfit and began to buy chunks of valuable property in the financial district.

Bowes was still under 30 when he became a member of the Grand Jury in 1904. He promptly waged a war on civic crime and corruption that paved the way for the sensational graft trials that later ripped the city.

The affluent young man next decided to make the Grand Tour and returned from Europe in time to join the fashionable throng rapturously listening to Caruso sing on the night of April 17, 1906.

The next morning San Francisco lay in ruins . . . and so did Bowes' fortune.

He stuck around just long enough to pay off his debts, and then hit for Tacoma. Before you can spell "m-o-n-e-y" he was doing great again.

In the winter of 1909 he also acquired a lovely wife, the talented actress Margaret Illington, three days after her divorce from the renowned theatrical producer Daniel Frohman.

This happy union, which lasted until she died in 1934, presaged his highly successful amalgamation of real estate and show business.

The rank "major," incidentally, was an honorary title bestowed on him by the Adjutant General's office in recognition of his work as a $1-a-year man during World War I.

(He was an honorary brigadier general and lieutenant colonel in three states and an honorary colonel in four, too.)

Bowes built show houses in Boston and New York. Then, in 1918, he hit his stride and achieved national renown when he constructed the Capitol Theater in Manhattan.

Early in the '20s he also assumed direction of a folksy radio program, called "Major Bowes' Capitol Family," which eventually spawned his roaringly successful, if consummately corny, amateur hour.

An ardent student of Napoleon, Bowes soon ruled an empire of his own, which extended into the motion picture industry and included the vice presidency of Metro-Goldwyn-Mayer.

By 1930 he was master of "Laurel Hill," a magnificent estate overlooking the Hudson at Ossining, N.Y., that boasted a lake and 15 waterfalls on the extensive grounds. In the mansion hung an impressive art collection, including works of Whistler, Sargent and Duveneck.

When the house and everything in it burned seven years later, he acquired another domain in New Jersey as well as a smart Manhattan apartment and an 81-foot yacht.

The fortune of this South-o'-the-Slot-reared lad at the time of his death in 1946 was close to $3.5 million.

The Rise and Fall of Johnny Skae

E VER HEAR of Johnny Skae? Probably not.
Nevertheless, he was a multimillionaire at one point.
Amassed them in a short time, too, without much effort. But,
as they say, easy come, easy go.

A native of Canada, Johnny came to San Francisco as a
boy and learned to be a telegraph operator.

He got a job with the California Telegraph Company around
the time the Fabulous Four were starting to develop the vast
resources of the Comstock Lode.

Operating quietly in Virginia City, John Mackay and Jim
Fair were in constant touch with their partners, Bill O'Brien
and Jim Flood, in San Francisco.

In order to keep secret the real state of affairs until they
were ready to spring it on the public, the quartet sent their
communications in code.

Johnny, usually on the receiving end of the Nevada wire,
succeeded in deciphering the messages, and so learned of the
preliminary movements of the great bonanza several days before the exciting news broke.

So he invested all his cash in the Virginia Consolidated and
California mines and, in exchange for tipping off his brokers,

managed to acquire additional huge blocks of stock on margin, paying from $20 to $30 a share.

He continued to buy heavily even after the price rose.

Finally, when it reached $1000 and the tidal wave began to recede, Johnny was worth over $3 million.

By this time he'd given up his job and was a familiar, envied figure on the S.F. Stock Exchange.

Moving to Nevada, where he assumed control of the Virginia and Gold Hill Water Works, he lived it up, threw his money around like confetti and entertained like a maharajah.

His trout breakfasts, at which he served the finest imported vintage wines, were famous.

A story goes that he lost $60,000 in a poker game one night.

Presumably believing that his luck would hold, Johnny went on speculating.

He bought 8000 shares and had himself made president of the Sierra Nevada mine, which was way down on the market and gave no indication of proving productive.

Meanwhile, no longer in a strategic position, Johnny had no way of knowing about the intricate, inside machinations of the Con. and Cal. hierarchy and didn't unload in time.

As with hundreds of others, his stock was steadily being gobbled up by the big wheels of that operation.

In 1878 came a sudden depression all along the Comstock, and Johnny, his fortune greatly decreased, left for the East to find other fields of endeavor.

En route he learned that a bonanza seemed likely at the Sierra Nevada, rushed back and began buying like crazy again, mostly on margin. The stock rose from 50 cents to $273 a share.

His holdings amounted to $10 million—on paper at least— and once more our boy was the lion of the hour, hailed as "the father of the new bonanza."

But the bonanza was a bust. Came another crash and Johnny went broke with it.

For a spell thereafter he worked as a bookkeeper in a small-pox hospital, then disappeared.

In 1884 he was picked up as a common drunk on a San Francisco street. At the police station he didn't have the necessary five dollars to post bail.

A few months later he was dead.

IV

Tragedies

The Angel in White Plotted Murder

T HE PRINCIPALS in the cast of one of San Francisco's celebrated murder cases were Francis Joseph Morgan Grace,
60-ish, frail of frame and ailing, and Frieda Augusta Wilhel-
mina Weltz, a robust trained nurse in her early 40s.

Grace was the grandnephew of W. R. Grace, founder of
the steamship line, and a clubman of note.

His wife, also a semi-invalid, had been Theodosia Cook,
the granddaughter of David Colton, an associate of the
railroad-building Big Four—Crocker, Stanford, Hopkins and
Huntington.

The couple maintained a smart 10-room penthouse on the
roof of the Alexander Hamilton Hotel which had a private
entrance and was staffed with its own servants.

They also had an impressive country place, called "The
Cabins," at Santa Cruz, where, since Grace's retirement, they
spent much time.

Frieda, who stemmed from Pennsylvania Dutch stock, had
served as an Army nurse during World War I. She had been
employed by Grace, who seemed to have had a succession
of ministering angels in starched white uniforms.

In fact, one of them, described as an attractive demi-blonde, about 28, was sitting on a lawn swing with him in the gardens of the Santa Cruz place on the fateful afternoon of September 9, 1933.

Frieda had been discharged some 18 months earlier and for a large part of that time, it later became known, she had been stalking Grace in town and country.

It had been her custom, for instance, to alternate between front rooms of a hotel and lodging house directly across from the Grace estate and therefore conveniently located for checking the action at The Cabins.

Immediately after she'd seen his wife and a friend leave the house that day, she scurried over. Grace walked to the edge of the lawn alone and spoke briefly with her before a shot rang out. He staggered into the residence and collapsed, dying, in the hall. The butler, who'd been in the kitchen, rushed to the front door, saw his employer in a pool of blood and the nurse struggling for the gun with his assailant.

After she was disarmed, Frieda whipped something out of her purse, popped it into her mouth and washed it down with a sip of water from a nearby birdbath. She then promptly fell into a swoon and still was more or less out of it when she was packed off to jail.

She maintained that she knew what she had done, that she had done it for a good and sufficient reason, which she would not divulge even to her most intimate friend, but one that had nothing to do with romance.

When the trial started a couple of months later, however, Frieda changed her story. While she was in his employ, the elderly, frail Grace had drugged and attacked her, she said.

Her health had been impaired. Although she had asked Grace that day for the modest sum of $300 to finance medical care and perhaps a nice rest, too, he had spurned and struck at her.

But she had no intention of killing him—just herself. The gun had gone off accidentally.

The deceased's current nurse, eyewitness to the shooting, shot holes in much of this testimony. It was proved, too, that Frieda had threatened Grace with a pistol on other occasions. Also brought out was the fact that the defendant was not destitute, had many relatives and devoted friends and money in the bank besides.

Furthermore, because of her service with the Army in World War I, she was entitled to treatment in a Government hospital. The prosecution suggested that unreasonable jealousy could have been the motive for the crime.

The death penalty was demanded. Things didn't look good for Frieda.

The jury consisted of 11 men and one woman. They deliberated 11 hours and took five ballots. When they reached an agreement, the woman juror, who chivalrously enough had been elected foreman, stood up and loudly and clearly pronounced the words "Not Guilty!"

Then she dashed from the box and rushed over to embrace Frieda. They wept in each other's arms, while the packed house of spectators cheered.

The Star Fell in San Francisco

A SAN FRANCISCO scandal that ricocheted like angry lightning
across the nation followed the death in September, 1921,
of Virginia Rappe, a film bit player, and left in its wake the
wreckage of the career of one of motion pictures' most successful early stars, Roscoe (Fatty) Arbuckle.

The king-sized comedian, who started his career here, was
arrested for the girl's murder. The charge later was reduced
to manslaughter.

It was a messy business and for weeks the lurid details were
splashed over countless newspaper columns across the country.

Briefly—the young actress had been found writhing in agony
on a bed in Arbuckle's suite at the St. Francis Hotel after
a wild drinking party he had hosted. She died a few days
later in a local hospital.

The rotund actor, for diverse reasons, was held responsible.

The sensational tragedy proved particularly shocking to the
public, who had adored what they had thought of merely as
a funny, good-natured, obese boy.

(It's said that he weighed 15 pounds at birth and 185 when
he was 10 years old.)

He ranked second only to Charlie Chaplin as a laugh-getter in the affections of the fans, who had roared at his antics in his always clean, if slapstick, comedies.

Hollywood, too, was horrified, and immediately four of his films, ready for release and representing an investment of hundreds of thousand of dollars, were shelved.

Arbuckle's estranged first wife rushed to his side and a battery of top-ranking lawyers was lined up to plead his case.

The trial dragged on for seven months while 65 witnesses, many from far afield, took the stand in his defense. The comedian's considerable fortune gradually dissolved.

Finally in April, 1922, the jury brought in a verdict of not guilty and he was acquitted.

But he was not exonerated in the minds of the people, who, bitter at the shattering of an idol, never forgave him.

Moreover, exhibitors banned his films. Although most of his friends in the colony remained loyal, the moguls of the picture industry turned their backs on him.

Subsequently this attitude was relaxed somewhat, and he was granted a "pardon" by the then film censor-czar, Will Hays. But nothing helped to remove the scurrilous stain and he sank into comparative obscurity.

(Even the St. Francis suffered a stigma due to the glare of unwelcome publicity, which took a long time to dissipate.)

Arbuckle, a movie pioneer who'd begun his film career in 1913, was finished.

For a while after the furor died down he managed to secure an occasional nightclub engagement—leading an orchestra, singing or dancing—and he also directed a couple of films, hiding behind the pseudonym "Will B. Good"!

Eventually he left Hollywood to try to make a comeback in the East, and in 1927 he was signed by an independent producer to appear in a series of comedies filmed in Europe.

As time rolled on his wife divorced him. He remarried and

was divorced for the second time. Then in June, 1932, Fatty married Addie McPhail, who was appearing with him in a vaudeville sketch.

Almost a year to the day later, she found him dead in bed in their New York hotel room, presumably the victim of a heart attack at the age of 46. His body lay in state in the same funeral chapel that had been the scene of a riot a few years earlier when the remains of the great Latin lover, Rudolph Valentino, were displayed.

Manhattan police had braced themselves for a similar hysterical onslaught, but only a few hundred of Arbuckle's one-time millions of admirers walked by the casket and there were no demonstrations.

The Maid Was Mad

C FREDERICK KOHL, thanks to Adele Verge, had no chance of becoming a merry old soul.

In 1904, a few years before Adele was to enter his life, Frederick, a wealthy San Francisco business leader, had married a charming blonde Washington, D.C. belle named Mary Elizabeth Godey, whose intimates called her Bessie. They took their place in the forefront of San Francisco society but their pleasant, gilt-edged existence was not destined to last.

Deciding to spend part of the winter of 1909 in the Southern California town of Riverside, they engaged rooms at a fine hotel there and took with them Mademoiselle Verge, a maid who had been hired in France by Kohl's mother on a trip abroad.

After she had slapped a chauffeur, slugged a clerk, and spat in the faces of several people, Kohl decided that she was not an ideal employee. Frank A. Miller, the hotel's proprietor, heartily concurred. Adele's irrational actions, he said, had been terrifying staff and guests alike. Something had to be done.

Something was. They had her taken into custody and placed under observation. Although one of the examining physicians pronounced her insane and possibly dangerous, other doctors didn't agree, and after a hearing she was released.

Adele spurned the Kohls' offer to pay her way back to France, hired a lawyer and proceded to sue both Kohl and Miller for slander, malicious persecution and false arrest, asking $30,000 damages from each.

Almost two years elapsed before the trial was held in 1911 in San Francisco. The jury failed to agree and the case was dismissed. Adele had lost.

Furious, she rushed out of the courtroom ahead of the defendants and waited for them with pistol in hand. When Kohl appeared, she shot him in the chest. "I knew it would come to this," he said before collapsing. Miller scampered out of range.

Adele wept and wailed from jail that she didn't know why she had done it and claimed she had only defended herself after being attacked by hoodlums hired by Kohl.

Porter Ashe, a renowned criminal lawyer of the era, came to her rescue. He saw to it that instead of being tried for attempted murder she was committed to a state mental institution. Not long after she was deported to her native land as an undesirable, where she was promptly incarcerated again.

With his recovery, Kohl's memories of Adele gradually began to recede. But then his marriage slowly soured.

Only a few years after they completed a magnificent Burlingame estate the Kohls parted permanently, although they were never to be divorced. The beautiful Bessie left California and divided her time between New York and Europe.

Conceivably the mad Adele was to some extent responsible, for Kohl had become a harassed, haunted man, withdrawn, morose and moody. She had escaped from the French asylum after carving up a guard and had begun to bombard Kohl with notes promising him a similar fate.

When they began to be stamped "Vancouver, B.C." the thoroughly alarmed recipient requested help from the authorities. Adele was arrested and placed in a Canadian hospital in 1921—10 years after the near-fatal shooting.

Meanwhile Kohl had found solace with Mrs. Marion Louderback Lord, a stunning, mature divorcee. Present always, though, was the nerve-wracking possibility that Adele, so adept at eluding her keepers, might return.

November, 1921 found Kohl ill, weak and apprehensive, seeking respite at fashionable Del Monte Lodge on Monterey Peninsula's Pebble Beach. Shortly after 8 o'clock on the morning of the 23rd his valet awakened and dressed him and ordered breakfast sent to his room.

Kohl ate the meal alone. Then two hours later, without rising from the table, he shot himself through the head. His will, filed a week after the suicide, left most of his considerable fortune to Marion Lord.

Undoubtedly anticipating trouble, he had stipulated that Mrs. Lord receive $250,000 outright until the estate was settled. He offered his wife the same amount, or $1000 a month for life or until she remarried. A gaggle of relatives, some of them real, tried to break the will—all to no avail. Bessie, while less than jubilant, decided to take the lump sum.

Mrs. Lord didn't stick around for the court battles that continued until May, 1923. She put her affairs in the hands of competent attorneys and left for Paris.

Adele Verge was back in Europe, too—and on the loose. For several years after Kohl's death she kept complaining about being menaced by his hired guns.

Sometimes, she said, they even sprayed her lodgings with deadly gas.

The Story of a Mad Mama

Lᴉᴋᴇ ᴀɴʏ other city, San Francisco has had its share of shocking affairs.

One that set the townspeople vibrating during the champagne days of the early '90s had all the best dramatic ingredients—illicit love, madness and murder.

Heading the cast of characters were Truly Shattuck, a beautiful and popular actress, and her lover, Harry Poole, a handsome 23-year-old man-about-town believed to have been the prospective heir to a sizable fortune.

The villainess was the girl's domineering mother, Mrs. Jane Shattuck.

Born Estullia Boucharde in San Miguel, Truly was a luscious, dark-eyed cupcake who didn't hesitate to wear pink tights and display a figure ample enough to suit the masculine taste of the time.

She had met Poole in 1892. He was a prominent member of the National Guard, she was Sweet Sixteen and a shopgirl—just before she joined the chorus line at the old Tivoli Theater.

Their romantic path had been rocky, though, and on New Year's Eve 1893 they quarreled and parted. Truly promptly signed up with a theatrical company to go on the road.

But Poole, whom her mother disliked as she did any and all of her daughter's suitors, persuaded Truly to dine with him the following Saturday evening at the Cliff House.

They made up over the entree and by the time dessert was served decided to be married secretly the following Monday.

Then they celebrated the decision by spending the rest of the night together.

It wasn't until 9 o'clock on the Sabbath morn that Truly returned home and was greeted by her irate mother who demanded to know if she were married. Truly said no but demurely announced that she would be the next day.

Mama went into hysterics and collapsed on her bed. She pulled herself together long enough however to insist that Truly write Harry a note at her dictation saying that her mother was dying and urging him to come post haste for a deathbed reconciliation.

The letter was dispatched by messenger.

Poole came on the double. There was mama still in bed but by no means breathing her last. In fact she had plenty of lung power to berate him and insisted that he marry her daughter immediately—*that day.*

The young man tried to explain that as it was Sunday no license could be secured but mother ignored him, tossed on her pillows and continued to rant.

At this point Truly feeling the need for refreshment went into the kitchen for a glass of water—whereupon bang-bang: mother shot and killed Poole!

Spectators nearly tore the courtroom apart when the case came to trial. Truly, always in attendance, never looked lovelier. She blushed prettily when her torrid love letters to Harry were read aloud and fainted conveniently when asked pertinent details about her affair with the deceased.

Mother's defense had been that Poole had done her beautiful baby wrong.

Nevertheless the jury brought in a guilty verdict and she was sentenced to life imprisonment in San Quentin.

But after an appeal a new trial was granted. This time Mrs. Shattuck was acquitted.

Meanwhile the sensational publicity all over the nation helped Truly's career to zoom and in 1895 at the age of 19 she was the most celebrated woman in San Francisco.

She went on to more triumphs, marriage and divorce. By the time she was 34 Truly hit the skids. She opened a hot dog stand in Hollywood—picking a spot near a studio in hopes of catching a director's eye. But she was finished. And there in 1954 she died—61 years after her mother had put a period to poor Poole.

The Pistol-Packing Socialite

THE ANNALS of San Francisco society contain no story more fascinating, sensational—or gruesome—than that of a beautiful woman named Mary Crittenden Scott, the daughter of Henry H. Scott, a prosperous local merchant and one-time Deputy Collector of Customs.

Mrs. Monroe Salisbury, sometimes called "Queen of The Fortnightlies" (an exclusive dancing group), was her aunt, and she was related to the Boardman, Keyes and other prominent families.

Furthermore she was supposed to be kin to President Benjamin Harrison.

At a fancy wedding in the late '90s Mary married Neville H. Castle, a promising young attorney.

The couple established themselves in a suite at the Hotel Vendome in San Jose, where Castle went into practice.

The attractive young matron acquired something of a social leader's reputation in the Garden City when she organized a series of private subscription "hops" at her hotel.

Her guest list presumably was selected by whim, as, for reasons best known to herself, Mary omitted the names of many who felt they should have been included.

So it wasn't long before a furious social tempest started blowing, with Mary in the middle.

Meanwhile, due undoubtedly in some degree to her arbitrary wounding of influential feelings, Castle's law practice wasn't prospering.

Then Mary really rocked her friends with the announcement that she was going on the stage. She joined Tim Frawley's famous company, then performing in San Francisco's old California Theater in "The Princess and the Butterfly."

Society recovered long enough to turn out in full force for her debut. Missing from the audience, though, was Mr. Castle, who by this time had run aground financially and left San Jose to seek his fortune in the Klondike.

Her engagement ended, Mary lit out for New York and there appeared briefly in vaudeville.

Chic and charming though she was, Mary's dramatic career languished. Moreover, the suspicion that more than miles separated the Castles became a certainty with the news in August, 1909, that Mary had shot a man and was in jail.

Interest in the case was heightened further by the fact that her target, William D. Craig, a wealthy lawyer, also was from San Francisco.

In front of the old Waldorf Astoria Hotel around 5 o'clock, Mary had approached Craig and suggested a little chat.

But he brushed her aside. So she followed him into the famed marble and gilt Peacock Alley. He hurried into an elevator—but not fast enough.

Mary rushed in after him, pulled a pistol from her purse and fired pointblank.

Although Craig crashed against a wall, he didn't fall, nor was there any sign of blood. Mary was about to have another go at him when a house detective leaped through the crowd, disarmed her and yelled to the operator to take the car up.

There had been nothing the matter with Mary's aim, incidentally. It was straight to the heart. But she had been foiled by a fountain pen and a handkerchief in Craig's vest pocket.

Mary and Craig were taken to jail; the lovely assailant giving the performance of her life. Her alternate swoons and hysteria were accompanied by protestations of Craig's wrong-doings.

When Mrs. Craig was notified by phone, she said that both she and her husband had befriended Mary and that this surely was a fine way to repay their friendship.

Mary trembled and swayed toward Craig as she asked him not to prosecute her because she didn't mean it. Ducking out of range, Craig said he darn well was going to.

Mrs. Castle spent six days in jail before her $3000 bail was raised. And she made the most of every minute.

Mary had been heard to say several times that she was punishing him for doing her wrong but her story subsequently changed. She intended to shoot herself, she maintained, and Craig had told her to go ahead and do it. But as she was about to, he grappled with her for the gun and it had gone off accidentally.

Furthermore, she asked, what gave anybody the notion that she had been pursuing him? Why, he had been pestering her, and she was afraid he would compromise her good name.

Craig, on the other hand, insisted that Mary had been a thorn in his flesh for a long time and he was firmly convinced she was off her rocker.

His wife bolstered this theory and said that although the three had been friends since childhood in San Francisco, Mary recently seemed to be "insane on the subject of possessing her husband."

Mary threatened that once this phase was past *she* would file serious charges against Craig.

Finally the assailant's army officer brother arrived in New York and persuaded Craig, after a series of chats, to forget the whole thing. So when the case went to the grand jury the next month it was dismissed. Mary didn't follow through with any accusations against Craig, either.

Meanwhile, up in Alaska her spouse, Mr. Castle, was prospering. There in October of the same year he filed for divorce on the gentlemanly grounds of desertion. The final decree was awarded the following January.

So Mary, now nearing 40, was free to marry again. And that she promptly did in March. Porter Charlton, her bridegroom, was the son of a prominent Nebraska jurist and barely 21 years old.

Early in April the couple sailed for Italy on a projected lengthy honeymoon. Some of Mary's kinfolk in San Francisco received letters from Charlton, whom they had never seen, reporting that he and Mary were as happy as "two cooing doves."

But on June 9 the lines of some fishermen tangled with a heavy object in Lake Como, which proved to be a trunk weighted down by a large rock and bound securely with stout rope. Jammed inside was the body of a badly beaten woman.

The horrified men reported their grisly find to the carabinieri, who, through sheaves of letters, photographs and other personal belongings also in the trunk, easily identified the cadaver as Mary Charlton. (An autopsy showed that she had still been alive when the trunk had been dropped into the lake.)

Her youthful spouse was missing, too, and at first it was assumed that both had met with foul play. But that notion soon was dispelled.

A hotel keeper in Como said that he'd been forced to evict them, as their constant violent quarrels, interspersed with boisterous parties, had disturbed the other guests.

The Charltons then leased a villa from its Russian owner at a distance from the town.

Finally someone remembered having seen the slim, blonde bridegroom leave the village at night carrying a valise.

A search for him started all over Europe. However, Mary's brother, H. H. Scott, acting on a hunch, decided to check the passengers on all incoming steamers at Hoboken. He hit pay dirt the first day.

Charlton had sailed for the U. S. from Genoa under an assumed name. Scott spotted him and a full, signed confession was extracted at the police station. Mary, he explained, had been taunting him for being the all-around champion lousy husband, so in a rage he had let her have it with a wooden mallet.

He had then stuffed her still-breathing body into a trunk (first removing a few trinkets of jewelry) and thrown it into the famed lake, where it had been found by the fishermen.

Although insisting that he was "bereft of his senses" at the time of the homicide and couldn't even remember the exact date, he managed to recall other details vividly. His father, Judge Paul Charlton, immediately sought the release of his 21-year-old son on grounds of insanity.

Italy demanded that Charlton be returned and held for trial there. His extradition was fought clear up to the U.S. Supreme Court. Not until the end of August, 1913, was the culprit returned to the scene of his crime.

His trial began at last on October 5, 1915. On the 25th, Charlton, who had signed a full confession over five years earlier, was found guilty.

But the jury took the view that he was "only partially responsible, that there were extenuating circumstances and great provocation" and, besides, held a generally indulgent attitude towards crimes of passion. He was sentenced to just six years and eight months imprisonment.

Moreover, due to amnesty, Charlton actually had to serve only 29 days!

Tale of the Strange Sisters

WHILE cleaning out a desk, a reader came upon a picture postcard that stirred memories of a bizarre tale of two sisters spiced with scandal, tragedy, touches of terror as well as a soupcon of high society.

The photo—presumably taken sometime before 1916—shows Ella May Clemmons and Wong Sun Yue in their combined tearoom and curio shop in Chinatown.

The story begins in the '80s when Ella May and her older sister Katherine came to San Francisco from the Midwest with their parents.

Katherine, a big, buxom blonde beauty, worked in a milliner's shop for a spell before going on the stage. She caught the roving eye of Buffalo Bill Cody and he invited her to join his troupe. She made a world tour with Buffalo Bill and took the plump, mousey Ella May along as chaperon.

But the sisters had a falling out in New York in 1897. Ella May returned to San Francisco while Katherine remained in the East to hit the matrimonial jackpot. She became the wife of Howard Gould, one of the sons of the fantastically rich Jay.

Meanwhile Ella May labored at a number of modest jobs

in San Francisco. She waited on table, demonstrated food products and even sold newspapers on the street.

But she was given to good deeds and devoted most of her time and money to a sort of kindergarten in Chinatown, teaching youngsters religion and reading in a building that became known as "The Little House of Gold."

Enter now Wong Sun Yue, a kindly, ineffectual Chinese with an enormous appetite for opium. Ella May decided that her main mission in life hereafter was to cure him of his addiction. She did not marry him, as was generally believed, for the excellent reason that he already had a wife in China. They did, however, set up housekeeping together and opened the shop at 897 Sacramento street.

They got a lot of publicity too, thanks to the Gould connection and the curious beat a path to their establishment.

Ella May's outraged mama disowned her. The Goulds—after failing to pass Yue off as "an aristocratic merchant prince"— were furious.

About this time Katherine and Howard became embroiled in divorce proceedings and Gould detectives attempted to obtain derogatory information about Katherine from her sister. Gould's men offered substantial amounts of money if she'd cooperate. Although the two had not seen eye-to-eye for some time, Ella May refused to turn on her sister.

Perhaps in return for her loyalty, Katherine, who in 1907 had managed to obtain a satisfactory settlement from her spouse, financed a trip to the Orient for herself, Ella May and Yue.

Discord again darkened the scene. Katherine returned to the U.S. in a huff. Yue returned to his wife and, after nursing some charges through smallpox, poor Ella May finally made it back to San Francisco.

Katherine died in 1930 and willed Ella May, by then pushing 60, around $80,000 and several items of valuable jewelry—a fact that was to seal her doom.

Taken ill, Ella May consulted Hjalmar Groneman, billed as a "drugless physician" but actually a quack, and from then on was in his power.

He prescribed equal parts of strenuous diet and rigorous exercise for the ailing Ella May but she gradually grew worse.

Then in September 1935, just nine days before she died, Ella May (who was in a coma most of the time) and Groneman were married.

It wasn't until the bridegroom claimed her estate that Ella May's few friends learned of her death and alerted the authorities.

Suspecting foul play or at least criminal negligence, a grand jury indicted Groneman for manslaughter.

But the lady who was to have been the principal witness at the trial vanished.

So the case against Groneman collapsed and he collected all of Ella May's property.

The Tragic Trip of Mrs. Stanford

JANE LATHROP STANFORD, widow of Leland Stanford, one-time Governor, U. S. Senator and railroad tycoon, left San Francisco for Hawaii on February 9, 1905, "in hopes of improving her health." That was the reason given the public for the trip, and, in a manner of speaking, it was true.

For during the previous month someone presumably had tried to poison her.

Guards had been placed in her Nob Hill mansion while an investigation was underway and the naturally-upset Mrs. Stanford spent a few days in San Jose and later at the St. Francis Hotel with her long-time confidential secretary, Bertha Berner. Friends then advised her to leave town for a while.

This startling episode was the curtain raiser for a mystery that rocked the nation and marked the beginning of the University cofounder's final days.

It had been Mrs. Stanford's custom to keep a bottle of mineral water in her bedroom. On the night of January 14 she drank half a glass at bedtime but, as the water tasted bitter, she promptly threw up.

(In her biography of Mrs. Stanford written nearly 30 years

later, Miss Berner said that her employer occasionally followed this practice when she felt she had eaten too much or something that didn't agree with her by "simply putting her finger down her throat.")

The contents of the bottle subsequently were analyzed and found to contain strychnine.

"Of course, consternation ruled," stated Miss Berner, adding the extraordinary comment: "But the belief was entertained that the Poland Water bottle had been used to hold some cleaning solution and taken to Mrs. Stanford's room by mistake."

Obviously, the police didn't share that belief. Members of the household staff were closely and lengthily questioned, although no arrests were made and, as far as we've been able to deduce, no satisfactory conclusion ever was reached.

The scene shifts now to Waikiki Beach, where Mrs. Stanford, her newly-engaged maid, May Hunt, and Miss Berner were staying at the Moana Hotel.

On February 28, Mrs. Stanford, feeling well and in a cheerful frame of mind, enjoyed a picnic with the two women. Mrs. Stanford ate a hearty lunch.

Returning to the hotel, she rested before having only a bowl of hot soup for dinner. Then, after a brief walk with Miss Berner, she retired to her room, where her secretary left her around nine o'clock.

Apparently feeling ill-at-ease, she took a laxative tablet and half a teaspoon of bicarbonate of soda before going to bed.

Versions of the events that followed differ only slightly. A man occupying the room next to Mrs. Stanford's told the press that he heard groans about 11 o'clock, entered the elderly matron's room and found her writhing on the floor in agony.

"I have been poisoned," he quoted her as saying. "They tried this once before. I came here to avoid them. This is a horrible death."

Miss Berner gives the impression she was the first to reach

Mrs. Stanford but admits she cried that she was poisoned.

"Putting my arm around her I led her into her room, of which the door was open."

Mrs. Stanford begged the house doctor to get a stomach pump and told a second physician who'd been called that only having her stomach pumped could save her.

But when the first doctor returned with the instrument his colleague wouldn't permit him to use it.

Seated in a chair before a hot-water filled wash basin in which she'd plunged her hands, Mrs. Stanford suddenly died. Her last words were: "May God forgive me my sins."

Investigation focused on the bottle of bicarbonate of soda. It contained traces of strychnine.

It was generally conceded that whoever had put the poison in the mineral water in San Francisco also had placed it in the soda in Honolulu.

The would-be assassin, if there was one, never was located and the case eventually was dropped.

A Chinese servant supposedly harboring a grudge against his employer; a disgruntled, discharged personal maid said to have been given to "spells of rage;" and a rather affluent former butler in whose home that lady then was living, were questioned.

The butler volunteered tales of intrigue among the servants and jealous feelings directed at Bertha Berner, Mrs. Stanford's confidential secretary for almost two decades, because she enjoyed an exalted position with special privileges.

He implicated Miss Berner, who'd accompanied Mrs. Stanford to Hawaii, in "graft," insisting that for many years she had shared with him rake-offs on large household purchases.

All suspected employees, however, soon were eliminated.

Meanwhile the body had been embalmed and a death mask taken. The autopsy was also under way, although results of the chemical analysis were slow in being made known.

Doctors were unable to isolate poison in the remains but

agreed that death was not due to disease. Furthermore, such symptoms as severe muscular rigidity and the violet color of the cadaver definitely indicated strychnine poisoning.

In the interim Dr. David Starr Jordan, president of Stanford University, and Timothy J. Hopkins, chairman of the trustees, both close friends of the deceased, accompanied by a couple of detectives they hired, sailed for the Islands.

Finally, on March 9 the coroner's jury, after deliberating less than two minutes, brought in this verdict:

"Death by poisoning, strychnine having been given with murderous intent by person or persons unknown."

The fact that private detectives had taken a long while to make their reports aroused suspicions that they were trying to cover up something, but this was emphatically denied.

Then after completing their investigation—"calling before them every person connected with the occurrence"—the detectives maintained they were fully convinced poisoning was *not* the cause of death.

On March 15, following a short funeral service in a Honolulu church, the casket was loaded aboard a ship and accompanied by all principals headed for San Francisco.

A large crowd had gathered at the pier—"the police far outnumbering the sightseers." The hearse, followed by the mourners' carriages, was escorted by a squad of mounted police to the railroad station at Third and Townsend streets, from which "all strangers were excluded."

Taken to her country residence in Palo Alto, Mrs. Stanford's body lay in state for three days although the coffin remained closed. Students conveyed the coffin from the church to the mausoleum.

Inscribed under her name on the vault was "Born August 26, 1828 in Mortality. Passed to Immortality February 28, 1905."

Vital organs had been brought back from Honolulu by Hopkins and Dr. Jordan and subjected to chemical, pathological and toxicological examination by several local physicians.

A summary of their carefully-worded, ambiguous report appears in Miss Berner's biography of Mrs. Stanford:

"From what is known of the effects of strychnine on the human body, there is no reason to believe that the death of Mrs. Stanford was due to the effect of a dose of strychnine, in itself not lethal, but determined in the direction of a fatal result of age and disease.

"There is no post mortem evidence that Mrs. Stanford died of strychnine poisoning. Consequently on the basis of data on hand the contention that Mrs. Stanford died of strychnine poisoning cannot be maintained.

"None of the symptoms observed before her death are incompatible with the assumption that she died of heart disease, in fact they are best explained by this diagnosis.

"It is our opinion, therefore, based upon the previous history of the deceased that the most probable cause of death was chronic myocarditis (chronic disease of the heart muscles resulting from partial obstruction of the blood vessels of the heart)."

Was Mrs. Stanford murdered?

Had she been poisoned with strychnine as she unquestionably believed, as also did the doctors involved in Hawaii and the coroner's jury?

Or was her death due to natural causes, as the group of San Francisco physicians maintained?

Could death have been due to a combination of circumstances heightened by hysteria and fright?

Is it possible that it could have been a grisly accident? Perhaps the strychnine, unaccountably placed in her bottle of bicarbonate of soda, had been designed for someone else?

Was the intended victim her long-time secretary-companion, Bertha Berner, of whom it's said that some of the household servants had been jealous?

If indeed Mrs. Stanford had been assassinated in the apparently second attempt on her life, who committed the crime and what was the motive?

Did a conspiracy to cover up and confuse exist? If so, why? To protect the deceased's good name?

The theory insisted upon by some closely connected with the Stanford estate was:

"Death caused by a surfeit of unsuitable food, unaccustomed exercise, unusual exposure during the picnic aggravated by other drugs in a medicinal tablet (a laxative), plus a small amount of strychnine in the soda."

But does it hold water?

True, according to Miss Berner's account of the fatal day in her biography of Mrs. Stanford, her employer had put away a hearty lunch, including a large slab of "soggy" gingerbread and several chocolate creams.

However, between lunch and the time she was taken ill— over 10 hours—she'd had only a bowl of clear soup. Moreover, the autopsy failed to discover any undigested food in the stomach.

There had been no "unaccustomed exercise or unusual exposure" during or after the outing—again according to Miss Berner, who spent the entire day and early evening with her mistress.

"Mrs. Stanford enjoyed the ride very much, sang on the way . . ." she wrote. "We found the picnic place a lovely spot . . . down from the highroad in a little grove on a level with the ocean not far distant.

"The coachman brought the carriage cushions and we seated Mrs. Stanford comfortably with a tree behind her to lean against. It was mild weather and she enjoyed the shade. . . .

"After 3 o'clock we got ready to return to the hotel. I gave

Mrs. Stanford my hand to help her rise but she found that she was quite stiff . . . calling for the maid, it took our combined efforts to get her up . . . her weakness may have been due to her unusual sitting position."

(Nothing extraordinary in this, surely, for a rather weighty woman of more than 76 years.)

"She was cheerful, saying repeatedly how much she enjoyed the day. . . ."

And one final query: Why did police drop the case?

The answer to that and all other questions may never be known.

The Bloody End of a Friendship

STATE SENATOR William I. Ferguson and George P. Johnston, clerk of the U. S. Circuit Court in San Francisco, were close friends.

Both were scholarly though convivial men, fond of society and great favorites with their associates.

When in an expansive mood, fun-loving Ferguson was given to song—delighting his cronies with amusing ditties.

Jovial Johnston, on the other hand, was prone to spout poetry—and is said to have been able to recite Scott's lengthy "Lady of the Lake" in its entirety.

These genial boys were whooping it up in a crowded San Francisco saloon on the night of August 19, 1858, when events suddenly took a nasty turn.

Johnston, a Southerner, accused Ferguson of having made some anti-slavery remarks at a political rally. This the latter hotly denied.

The conversation rapidly degenerated into a quarrel. Bystanders, sensing excitement, got into the act, took sides, and egged the pair on.

Before anyone could say "en garde," the opponents decided that the only way to settle the argument was on the field of honor.

This ridiculous conclusion was especially inane as, three years earlier, Johnston had urged the passing of legislation against dueling.

Anyhow, the men met on Angel Island two afternoons later.

The agreement was "pistols at 10 paces"—and if the first fire was ineffective, the distance was to be cut in half.

The original shots were without result, so they moved closer. Nothing happened on the second and third tries either.

Then Johnston demanded an apology or a fourth shot. Ferguson wouldn't bend, so they banged away again.

This time Johnston was hit on the left wrist and Ferguson on the right thigh.

Thereupon the principals expressed satisfaction and shook hands, and everyone returned to town. The fuss seemed to be over.

However, though Johnston's wound proved minor, Ferguson's was mortal, and he died September 14 while his leg was being amputated.

Johnston's trial was a travesty, and he was acquitted. A sensitive man, his real punishment lay in regret and sorrow for having been conned into shooting a friend.

Was It Tragedy or Fraud?

IN 1926 Aimee Semple McPherson dived into the sea off the Southern California coast and came up on the Arizona desert. Half a dozen years later Lee Schlesinger outdid the evangelist's remarkable feat by plunging into the Columbia River and emerging in South America.

After working at important posts in the Emporium, which his father then owned, and at the City of Paris, Lee, the oldest of four sons, was appointed vice president of another Schlesinger-controlled department store in Portland. He was in his early 30s, married and the father of two children.

About 11:30 one night in December, 1932, Lee vanished. The next day his sports car was located in 18 feet of water at the end of a dock. It was at first assumed that, confused by mist and rain, he had mistakenly taken a wrong road and crashed through a guard rail into the Columbia River.

Schlesinger wasn't found in the wreckage, however, giving rise to the belief that his body must have been thrown clear and taken downstream. So an intensive search began.

Almost immediately, though, it became apparent that all was not as accidental as it seemed and that even kidnapping was a possibility. A crudely written ransom note demanding

$30,000 was received by Schlesinger's socially prominent wife. This later proved to be a clumsy hoax. A couple of country characters told the police they had seen a man jump from an automobile just before hearing a loud splash. But their story fell apart under questioning.

An examination of the car showed that the hand throttle was wide open. One of the sheriffs on the case insisted right along that no one had been in the car when it took the dive.

Experts on the Columbia's currents maintained that a body couldn't have gone very far without being detected. There were rumors, too, that Schlesinger had been seen in various parts of the world. His father spent thousands of dollars running down each clue, no matter how tenuous.

Then, five months later, tragedy struck the family again, diverting attention from the mystery for the time being. Lee's younger brother, James William Lee Schlesinger (the two other brothers, Howard and Richard, also have "Lee" as middle names), committed suicide in Los Angeles by drinking whiskey laced with poison.

The following month, a body with a bullet hole in the head was fished from the Columbia. It matched in a general way the description of the missing man. But no member or representative of the family took the trouble to go north to view or assist in identifying the remains—a fact that caused considerable curiosity.

Meanwhile two insurance companies, on which Schlesinger held policies amounting to about a quarter of a million dollars, refused to pay off.

Marital difficulties to account for his disappearance were ruled out by his wife. But it was found that the missing man was heavily in debt and was being financially pressed.

Adding weight to the suspicion that all was not accidental, or even suicidal, was the fact that Schlesinger had made certain interesting preparations before he evaporated. For one thing, he had secured a passport and some visas to Far Eastern countries.

So the insurance company detectives belted on their trench coats and went to work. Schlesinger's trail led them around the world.

Instead of drowning, as at first was assumed, Schlesinger had shipped out of Seattle to Shanghai. From there his path was picked up in Hong Kong, Calcutta, Port Said and eventually Europe by way of the Suez Canal.

Then one day David Livingston, a lawyer for the wary insurance companies, was vacationing abroad and spotted Schlesinger on a Paris street. But Lee presumably saw him first and went into his successful vanishing act again.

The following December—almost two years since his first fade-out—he was discovered working for an import company in Buenos Aires and prospering, too.

He even had resumed his favorite sport of polo, although playing on borrowed mounts. The published news came as no surprise to his family and friends, who admitted that they'd been hearing from the prodigal son for some time.

Lee's wife, then living in Los Angeles, told the press that he had requested her to join him, but she was hesitating only because of their two children. When asked if she planned to secure a divorce, the reply was an emphatic "No!"

The lady exercised her woman's prerogative a few months later, however, and filed suit charging desertion.

A year and a half later Schlesinger, then making his home in Rio de Janeiro, acquired a new wife. He also got a new name.

It was Donald Moore, with "Lee" in the middle.

V

Palatial Places

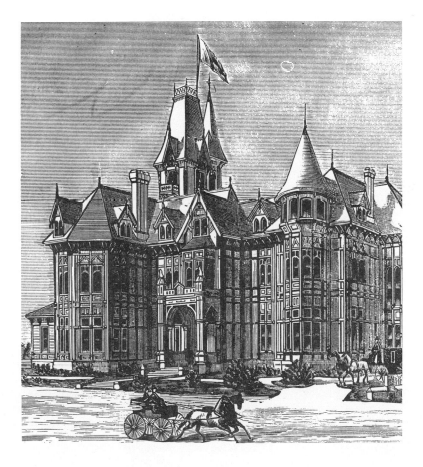

The Telegraph Hill Castle

THE TINY, two-story signal house atop Telegraph Hill, from which observers had reported the arrival of approaching ships, was built in September, 1849. This was blown down in 1870 and for the next dozen years the summit was bare.

Then in 1882 teams of horses began laboriously to drag loads of lumber up Filbert street and the construction of what was called a "German" castle was begun.

This was the grandiose project of Frederick O. Layman, who hoped to build a resort that might rival even the Cliff House in popularity. The place was a long, large wooden structure of more or less Gothic design with turrets and parapets. It contained a concert hall, a restaurant, a bar and a series of private dining rooms.

At one end was an observation tower that boasted a 50,000 candle-power lamp believed to have been the strongest light on the Pacific coast at the time. There also was a time ball, which dropped from a tall shaft at high noon.

But the place didn't catch on. For one thing, people complained that it was too inaccessible. So Layman organized a cable car company and tracks were laid from Powell street up the steep slope of Greenwich to the top. Service started in 1884.

Nevertheless, the customers continued to stay away. Then Adolph Sutro took over but even he couldn't make a success of it.

Under the later proprietorship of Duncan Ross, a noted swordsman, the establishment enjoyed some popularity for a while, principally because of the kind of medieval jousting exhibition he staged on Sunday afternoons.

Ross and a friend would dress in suits of armor, climb aboard horses and proceed to whack away at each other with broadswords. The onlookers were delighted but the clash of steel always scared the grazing goats which would scamper in all directions down the hill.

The final blow to the place was delivered when one of the cable cars, presumably overloaded, went out of control, tore down the slope and crashed, killing several passengers.

At any rate, Ross gave up. Thereafter it became successively the headquarters of an athletic club, a vaudeville theater, an art studio and eventually a cheap boarding house.

The Gray brothers, whose blasting of the hill left such horrendous scars, bought the castle around the turn of the century and used it as a dormitory for their workmen.

In July, 1903, a woman acquired it with plans to turn it into a tourist attraction. But five months later flames raced through the walls. Only one fire engine pulled by six horses was able to reach it—too late, however, to do any good.

Suddenly there was a tremendous crash and thousands of blazing cinders burst like a gigantic skyrocket.

Within a week a strong wind toppled what remained of the charred shell and that was the end of the ill-fated castle.

Music and Dance in the Wildwood

WHERE once rabbits rambled, now symphonies are played and grand operas performed. Where once coyotes slunk, now ballet and other dance troupes flit across an expansive stage.

That is an early-day capsule history of Sigmund Stern Grove.

It was in 1847 that George M. Greene, learning about the excellent farming and grazing land to be had for the asking on the Pacific Coast, left his home in Maine and with his wife headed west across the plains (or around The Horn, as some sources maintain).

They settled on a 160-acre homestead boasting a spring-fed lake abounding in ducks, in what today is the vicinity of 19th avenue and Sloat boulevard.

Soon George's brothers John and Alfred followed and took adjoining property. The latter ordered a house sent out from New England.

A son and namesake of George (a periodic prospector for both gold and oil, by the way) was born in Alfred's imported prefab dwelling.

It was George, Jr., who in his early 20's not only sowed Holland grass on the dunes to keep the sand from shifting but secured eucalyptus seeds from Australia and planted the towering trees that now form such an effective windbreak at the grove.

However, after they had been there a couple of decades a jurisdictional dispute stole into the clan's private paradise . . .

The Rancho de la Merced, a Spanish land grant in San Mateo county extending to about where Daly City is currently located, was acquired by one David Mahoney.

Now he had a trio of sharp lawyers who suggested he get the grant's boundaries extended farther north to encompass the Greene property.

Mahoney lost his case in the local courts, then appealed to the U.S. Supreme Court, which upheld it.

That made the Greenes technical squatters, and a U.S. Marshal called to tell them to pack up.

The fighting mad Greenes refused to budge, and backed up their stand by building a crude fort comprised of a wooden shed lined with metal, and told the so-and-sos to try to *make* them move.

Thereupon ensued several skirmishes involving gunplay, dynamite and even scalding water, but with no known serious casualties.

The Maine men, augmented by a Canadian lad who had fought with Custer, held the fort for three months.

Finally, in 1887, Congress passed a special act awarding the property to the Greenes, and Mahoney presumably retired to lick his legal wounds.

Five years later George Jr. decided to build a hotel on the land.

The reputation of the Trocadero Inn (as he named his hotel) has run the gamut from snow-white through lurid red to white again since it was built.

At the moment it's as pure as the driven snow. San Franciscans today know the place as the neatly painted house on the grounds of Sigmund Stern Grove.

At its inception the inn must have been a smart and highly respectable spot.

Besides the hotel proper, cabins were constructed and rented out to groups of the elite for weekend sojourns.

Multimillionaire timber tycoon C. A. Hooper, according to historians, was the first man to live at the resort for a while and in 1903 Adolph B. Spreckels operated it for a short period.

After that it was leased to Hiram Cook, under whose aegis it ran full blast.

He made major improvements—set up a dance pavilion and a beer garden, enclosed a deer park, provided rowboats for the lake and even a trout farm for unambitious anglers.

Nevertheless, one can only surmise that at this point the color of its repute must have started to take on a more vivid tinge and its clientele slipped into a gaudier category.

For Cook had been a prizefight referee and what was then called a man-about-town.

The shade certainly deepened right after the 1906 disaster, when at the climax of the era's political scandals Abe Ruef hid out and was taken into custody there by the authorities.

It continued in operation, however, for several years more, with Greene in charge.

But senior citizens will tell you that the roadhouse, set far back from the 19th avenue thoroughfare and discreetly hidden by trees, exuded a decidedly questionable odor. Finally it closed in 1916.

Greene, though, was still living in the house 15 years later, when the dwelling plus 12 acres were bought by Mrs. Stern and deeded to San Francisco to be used for recreational purposes in memory of her late husband.

Subsequently the house was renovated, the huge stage erected in the outdoor bowl, a prodigious amount of landscaping done, and between the city and Mrs. Stern the grounds grew to its present almost-100 acres.

The Saga of Peter Coutts

P ETER COUTTS, builder of Tower House at Stanford, wasn't really Peter Coutts.

The true name of this somewhat legendary Frenchman whose ghost has been said to stalk the campus, was Jean Baptiste Paulin Caporin, which he left behind in his native land when he came here but resumed when he returned.

Born in 1822 to wealthy, socially prominent parents who died when he was 20, Caporin used his considerable inheritance to enter the banking business. Later he became editor and publisher of *La Liberte*, an antiroyalist paper critical of Napoleon III.

Shortly before the Franco-Prussian War he invested five million francs in a venture in Alsace-Lorraine. This proved as disastrous as his political opinions. France lost that province to Germany and the stockholders held him personally responsible for the bank's losses.

So Caporin, apparently still wealthy, fled first to Belgium and then to Switzerland, where his aunt gave him the identification papers of his dead cousin, Peter Coutts. As Coutts he sailed for the U.S. in 1874 with his wife, their 11-year-old son and 5-year-old daughter and the children's governess, Eugenie Clogenson.

The party arrived in California in October that year and Coutts, as we must now call him, bought the some-1400-acre Matadero Ranch in the Mayfield area west of El Camino Real and began to build immediately.

By mid-summer of 1876 he had a showplace farm boasting of about 15 structures. There were stables for his prize-winning thoroughbred horses and a race track; barns for his herd of sleek Ayrshire cattle; kennels for blooded beagles, bunkhouses, a brick dairy, a water tower, a wincry—the works.

And, of course, there was the Tower House, now head-quarters of the Committee for Art at Stanford.

The family residence, subsequently dubbed Escondite Cot-tage (hiding place) by the late David Starr Jordan, Stanford's first president when he occupied it, was (and still is) an L-shaped wooden structure. Slightly remodeled, it presently serves as a student housing administration building.

The large rooms were filled with fine French furniture, and most of the redwood paneled walls were hung with French chintz in pastel shades.

Around the house extended a pretty garden with shade trees and a vineyard. There were also a fine park with an avenue of poplars, a small pine forest, and an artificial lake fed by a spring.

The lake was outlined with a cut stone wall and the little fern-fringed islands in it were connected with picturesque arched bridges, one of which remains, as do remnants of the rock work.

Frenchman's Lake, as students of the era who held rollicking commencement week gatherings there called it, lasted until 1922 when the university, considering it a health hazard, had it filled in.

It's believed that Coutts' ultimate intention was to build a mansion. In a futile effort to find an adequate water supply for future needs, he had several tunnels dug deep into the hills. This gave rise to rash of rumors—that they were shelters to protect him from possible enemies, and of buried treasure.

His political and other difficulties presumably resolved, in 1880 Coutts took his family back to Europe, never to return. Two years later he sold the Peninsula farm to Leland Stanford.

While Stanford was preparing to buy the estate in September, 1882, he instructed a representative of Coutts to make an inventory of the farm and dismiss all employees with the exception of "the two servant girls—Lizzie and the other," whose name apparently couldn't be recalled.

The transaction was completed in a London office on November 7 that year with Coutts and Eugenie Clogenson, his children's governess, signing the papers.

That requires a bit of explanation:

Coutts, who had come to the United States under his assumed name, had bought the land in 1874 as Coutts. Two years later, however, he made out a formal deed of sale to Mlle. Clogenson—which naturally started stories of an illicit romance.

He didn't record the deed, though, until 1879, shortly before leaving for abroad, and then only at the request of a Wells Fargo agent.

The complicated business probably was done as a safeguard against any possible creditors or enemies he had left in Europe.

Stanford paid $140,000 for the property. He promptly moved Coutts' cows out and his racehorses in using the place to raise thoroughbreds. It became known as the Running Farm, as opposed to the Trotting Farm, a mile away where he kept his trotters.

Meanwhile, Coutts, who had first gone to Brussels, went to Paris, where he maintained an impressive townhouse. He also had a magnificent castle at Evian les Bains and apparently didn't miss California at all.

He died in 1890 and is buried at Bordeaux.

A Lively Nob Hill House Warming

THE MARK HOPKINS, the hostelry which crowns Nob Hill, threw open its doors to the world in December, 1926.

The opening festivities were marked with a tour of inspection and a dinner party. Like many another housewarming, the affair was marred by a few minor incidents. For one thing, the brand-new stoves in the kitchen smoked badly. The smoke drifting toward the roof was tinted by the light from the red beacon that burns nightly, and gave the impression that the building was on fire.

No less than three separate alarms were turned in and, at three different times, the diners in the Peacock Court were treated to the sight of firemen toting heavy hoses bursting into the room.

Nervous owner George D. Smith and others of the hotel staff on each occasion cast anxious eyes toward the two huge tapestries, price-tagged $25,000, which decorated the walls. (During the various processes of face-lifting over the years, these tapestries have been banished to storage.)

Considering that so many people trooped through the hotel on that opening night, the souvenir-taking was negligible. Not that there weren't temptations. The dinner tables were set with sterling silver ashtrays, bread-and-butter plates and demi-tasse spoons. When the party was over the silver was counted, more than 50 spoons were missing.

Some of the guests apparently had been inadvertent thieves and taken the spoons in good faith, thinking they were meant to be mementos. One man even called up and said apologetically that three in his party had forgotten to take their spoons and would the management send them along, please?

The hotel also had difficulty in holding onto water lilies—wax ones. The paraffin posies used to float in the pool of the little "fountain lounge" between the lobby and the Peacock Court. This area later was to develop into that popular meeting spot, the lower bar, after the repeal of Prohibition. There had been no need for a bar then, as this was during those dreary dead days of alcoholic aridity.

Done in mosaic tile and filled with palms and ferns, it had an elegant, if definitely funereal, air. It was presided over by a nude woman, a marble maid.

The entire top floor was occupied by Daniel C. Jackling (the copper king) and his wife, who maintained a lavish apartment there for ten years. One day while the building was under construction, Mrs. Jackling expressed a desire to see the view from what was to be her home. Smith said that could be managed if she was game to ride up in one of those sideless, fresh-air elevators the workmen used. So together they took the windy journey up the naked steel girders to the highest point in San Francisco.

When the Jacklings decided to move permanently to their Woodside home, Smith did away with the apartment and carried out a long-cherished dream. He built a glass-enclosed skyroom. After much pondering upon a striking name for the top of the Mark, it was called just that.

The hotel is on the site of the many-turreted, gabled and cupolaed mansion constructed, but never occupied by, the man whose name it bears.

This Mark Hopkins is not to be confused with the Eastern educator. He was, perhaps, the best liked of the "Big Four," builders of the Central Pacific railroad—the others being Collis P. Huntington, Leland Stanford and Charles Crocker.

He was cautious and conservative, thrifty and prudent. He saved bits of string and horded odd nails and bolts. When he fished usable pieces of blotting paper out of wastebaskets in the railway offices, clerks were inclined to snicker behind their ledgers. But he was no miser, he simply hated waste.

After the general offices of the Central Pacific were moved from Sacramento to San Francisco in the early 1870s, Stanford and Crocker came down, too, and leased as pretentious houses as they could find while their huge homes on Nob Hill were being built.

"Uncle Mark," however, continued to prefer the simple life despite his mounting multi-millions. He had none of the vanity of his associates. He rented a small cottage for $35 a month on Sutter street near Leavenworth and tried to coax turnips and carrots to grow in his sandy backyard. He lived there five years. He kept no carriage. When the weather was good he walked to and from his office at Fourth and Townsend, and when it wasn't he rode the horse cars that went past his house.

Then his wife, Mary, who was about 20 years his junior, rebelled. She had no children and had devoted most of her time to her housekeeping and to avid reading—especially novels. Understandably enough, it annoyed her that her husband never took a vacation while his partners and their families made frequent trips to New York and Europe. What's more, Mary began to agitate about having a decent house of her own—one without a truck garden in the rear.

So her husband sighed, but decided to humor her. Besides which he saw a chance of making a sound real estate investment. Stanford had bought an entire block of land on the upper ridge of barren, windy Nob Hill, and Hopkins paid him $30,000 for the western half of it. Then came the problem of anchoring their houses. The partners turned the job over to the railroad's engineering staff, who enclosed the block bounded by California, Mason, Pine and Powell streets with a wall of slate-colored granite, remains of which may still be seen.

Hopkins gave his wife carte blanche on the architectural end of the house and she had a field day. It is said that Hopkins, while hoeing in his straggly Sutter street garden, would gaze up at the tremendous unfinished wooden mishmash which was to have been his home and wistfully ask anyone at hand whether they thought the "Hotel de Hopkins" would ever pay dividends. Seven different architects at one time worked on the monstrosity and the result was a gigantic jigsaw jumble.

But Uncle Mark was spared the ordeal of having to move into the eyesore and having to adjust himself to a more elaborate and complicated way of living. He died before the house was finished.

After Hopkins died, the house was lived in intermittently by the railroad builder's widow, Mary, a plump, colorless woman, retiring and square-jawed, about whom little was known. Soon the 50-year-old possessor of the Hopkins millions found herself the subject of innumerable newspaper articles, some factual, most fiction.

After one local sheet erroneously announced her engagement to a retired naval officer she left town in a huff following angry denials and settled in Great Barrington, Massachusetts. By this time the building bug had bitten her but good and she ordered a huge stone chateau constructed there. She also acquired a mansion in Manhattan and a couple of other places in the East.

As with the Nob Hill house, when it came to architects Mary thought several heads were better than one. So after hiring and firing three or four of them she finally permitted a 28-year-old decorator, Edward F. Searles, to finish the job.

When Mary returned to San Francisco, the townspeople

discovered she had changed. The mousy hausfrau had been replaced by a woman with dictatorial tendencies and an imperious manner. She was more than ever distrustful and uncooperative with the press. The more she dodged, the more was written. She grew bitter and suspicious and often quarreled with old friends.

Then Mr. Searles minced back into her life. His ruling passion was furniture and, as a representative of a New York decorating firm, he called on Mary to get a look at her tables and chairs. To the amazement of everyone concerned (especially her alarmed adopted son, Timothy Hopkins) Mary fell in love with Searles, 22 years her junior, and married him.

Three years later she died in the East and willed everything to her husband. Timothy, of course, sued to break the will. He didn't but it is reported that he received a large, out-of-court settlement.

Young Searles built a castle at Methuen, Massachusetts, constructed a great hall for a tremendous pipe organ, surrounded his property with a stone wall and became a recluse. He collected first editions into a valuable library and gathered works of art. He paid $250,000 for a statue of George Washington, for instance.

Death came to him in August, 1921 and he was buried in an elaborate tomb on his estate. Then *his* will caused a nationwide sensation. Searles left virtually everything to one Arthur T. Walker of whom no one, up to that point, had ever heard. Reporters located Walker, a clerk, living in Brooklyn. He didn't even have a telephone.

What's more he wouldn't talk and went into hiding after he gave the writers the slip.

But the bizarre business didn't end there. Two months after Searles's demise the District Attorney in his county received an anonymous letter to the effect that the millionaire had been poisoned. There were reports, too, that his body wasn't even on the property. But Searles was there all right. They dug him up one midnight. An autopsy proved, however, that he had died of natural causes.

So the obscure Walker, who had never owned a railroad tie, walked into Uncle Mark's millions.

The House was Jinxed

LEGENDS die hard—and people feel cheated when veils of secrecy are dissolved by simple reasonable explanations.

Thus it was that long after Mr. and Mrs. Alexander Russell revealed that they had nothing to hide in their large, brown, wooden residence at the beach, San Franciscans continued to call it The House of Mystery and whisper of eerie doings in the place.

The Russells had moved in the house set on a knoll facing the Great Highway between Ulloa and Vicente—on almost a square block of land—when the century was young.

The building had been put together in 1857 from the wreckage of a fine ship that foundered offshore. After having been used as disreputable tavern, it was deserted and remained a dilapidated derelict for almost three decades.

Then a wealthy man from Omaha spent thousands of dollars converting it into a handsome dwelling. When he left, the structure once again operated as a roadhouse for a brief period before the Russells took over.

Quite likely it was the tall fence they erected around the property to protect the gardens from sand and the stiff prevailing west wind that started the rumors.

Mrs. Russell, a dedicated student of philosophy who'd spent
much time studying religion in the Far East, had much Oriental art and furniture in the house, giving it an exotic air.

So the story circulated that the dwelling sheltered a strange
cult given to weird rites and ceremonials. Mrs. Russell was
said to have been called "Mother" by her disciples. Theodore
Wores' painting of the Kamakura Buddha, titled "The Light
of Asia," which she had bought for $5000 was said to hang
in a shrine.

These fanciful tales persisted even after Mrs. Russell granted
an interview to a reporter to set the record straight publicly.

She headed no cult, Mrs. Russell told the press, and therefore
there were no disciples. No one called her mother except
several children she had adopted.

Wores' celebrated picture was displayed, suitably enough,
in a room that contained only other Oriental things.

In November, 1910, a fire broke out in the adjoining garage
over which their two chauffeurs lived, and the building, plus
three cars, was demolished.

The Russells took the occasion to invite a few fire-watchers
into the residence, hoping in this way, perhaps, to dispel some
of the still rampant wild yarns. But the serenity they sought
was to be shattered tragically years later.

At midnight on Sept. 20, 1917, three physicians rushed to
the ocean front residence and found Mrs. Russell dead.

As the 52-year-old woman, usually described as radiant and
distinctive, had been in good health it was first assumed she'd
met with foul play.

But the circumstances of her death proved to be more bizarre.

That afternoon Mrs. Russell had undergone treatment for
the removal of wrinkles on her throat. Rita Kraus, a Post street
beauty operator, considered expert in this field, had done the
job.

The process involved burning the skin with a solution composed primarily of carbolic acid and Mrs. Russell had suffered severe pain. So a doctor who, it was said, "regularly cared᾿ for Mrs. Kraus' patients," was called.

After testing Mrs. Russell's heart he gave her a hypodermic injection of morphine for relief.

The medic stayed on for a couple of hours, and later testified that when he had departed around eight o'clock her pulse had been good and her breathing normal. He also left instructions that in an hour or so she was to be given a cup of strong black coffee as a "precuationary measure," explaining that the beverage would counteract the effects of the acid on her kidneys and nullify the morphine.

The orders weren't carried out, presumably because sometime between nine and 10 o'clock Mrs. Russell became desperately ill and the family physicians were summoned. They arrived, alas, too late.

After his wife's death, Russell moved out of the residence by the sea and much of the art treasures and furniture was sold.

The following summer he had a paralytic stroke and died the next year.

John Tait, a prominent restaurateur of the period, announced in February, 1919 that he was leasing the historic old place and would convert it into a smart cafe. And that he did.

There's never been a place in San Francisco quite like Tait's-At-The-Beach.

This cafe, restaurant, roadhouse or resort (it was called all four) converted from the Alexander Russell residence, had a certain cachet not approached by any similar establishment here before or after.

When, following a dozen years of operation, it folded due to the devastating effects of the Depression and Prohibition, the citizens were saddened.

John Tait had assembled exactly the right combination of

ingredients and in proper proportions when he leased the property in 1919. Throughout the '20s it was *the* place to go for socialites and celebrities.

Countless prominent personalities of the period, including a couple of U.S. Presidents, dined within this weathered wooden building.

The food was excellent, the service good, the bands played danceable music, and the atmosphere, though subdued, wasn't starchy.

The setting, of course, was responsible for a good deal of the pleasant aura. The house had been kept much as it was when the Russells were in residence. Tables of varying sizes were set in dark-paneled rooms, illuminated by flattering lighting and hung with fine paintings. The furnishings and objets d'art were tasteful—largely Oriental but not overwhelmingly so.

The surf crashing on the shore could be seen from the glass-enclosed porch. The sheltered garden contained a pavilion, winding paths and dwarfed trees.

But, alas, Tait eventually found he couldn't make the place pay and in 1931 the doors were padlocked.

Two years later it was reopened under new management and a new name—the Edgewater Beach Club. But things weren't the same by any means, and before long the police moved in and closed the club because of gambling.

Then on the sunny afternoon of Sunday, December 1, 1940 a fire of unexplained origin started in the tindery, dry structure occupied for several years only by a caretaker and his family.

An estimated 15,000 people in cars and on foot gathered to gawk as flames spurted, sparks showered like fireworks and smoke that could be seen for miles billowed from the building.

Thus, in a spectacular pyrotechnical display, the former House of Mystery burned to the ground.

VI

Unforgettable Characters

The Blacksmith's Odd Menage

SAN FRANCISCO may have had an edge on early-day characters, but it didn't have a monopoly.

While browsing one day we came upon the story of an
individual who, in matters of eccentricity, might have given
some of the raffish local boys a run.

He was called the Blacksmith, the only name he'd respond
to, although he never was known to engage in that trade.

He consistently refused to say where he was from or furnish
anything else about his past until the very end of his life,
and, even then, gave only a hint.

But that scrap of information was a shocker . . .

The Blacksmith's first appearance in California was in 1840,
when he arrived at the mission in San Rafael.

It was assumed that he had deserted some ship in San Francisco, but that was merely a guess.

He worked at various menial jobs for a few years in that
vicinity, and then vanished as suddenly and mysteriously as
he had appeared.

Next he turned up in the Bolinas area, which was beginning
to have a boom in the lumber business, though that isn't what

had attracted the stranger, for he made no effort to get into the act.

He converted a derelict hogshead that had been washed up on the beach into a "home," partly plugging the open end of the cask with a rock, in lieu of a door.

Apparently inured to all kinds of weather, he went about half-naked and always barefoot.

Food was no problem. He lived on fish and the abundant clams, and also managed to shoot some game with an antique flintlock musket from which the locks were long gone. (He discharged the ancient weapon by lighting a match to the powder in the pan.)

Lacking a boat he made a small raft and used to propel it around Bolinas Bay with a long pole.

He shunned his fellow man, but had two devoted four-footed friends—a cat and a pig—that followed him everywhere he went.

So great was their affection for the Blacksmith that if he chanced to push off from shore without inviting them along, the strangely assorted pair would plunge into the water and swim out to him!

Presumably he doted on bonfires and day or night, winter or summer, when and wherever he'd stop on his peregrinations, he'd build large, roaring ones and sit beside them.

Later, when a trading post was established on the point, he frequently dropped in to acquire a supply of whiskey and return to his shelter to get gloriously drunk.

Which brings up a little trick he played one day after he'd arrived to buy some grog, found the store closed and all the inhabitants gone.

The old codger took revenge for his disappointment by pouring out all the sweet water on the premises and replacing it with salt water.

He also emptied the only small spring and filled that, too, with the briny.

Few meals were enjoyed in Bolinas that night.

In 1857, he became desperately ill. As it was apparent the end was near, a few of the more curious citizens tried to pry loose some facts.

But he refused to give any details except to intimate that he had murdered his wife!

On a hill overlooking the little bay they buried the Blacksmith, a character unsung and unloved—except by a cat and a pig.

She Even Joined a Harem

No REMINISCENCES of local ladies who have married titles would be complete without mention of the late Princess Alexander Galitzine who began life as Aimee Crocker. She was the daughter of Judge and Mrs. Edwin B. Crocker of Sacramento whose old home now is an art gallery, and she inherited millions.

Aimee was an uninhibited spirit whose sensational escapades were shockers in her day and certainly wouldn't go unnoticed even in this free and easy era. She had five husbands and many romances but still found time for performing as a veiled Oriental dancer in a supper room, writing a couple of books including a frank autobiography and giving exotic parties on two continents. She hunted big game in India alone with only a guide when a woman was considered a hussy if she didn't ride side-saddle in the park. She is said to have spent three weeks in a Turkish harem on a dare.

Even the circumstances of her first marriage, which took place in her teens, are highly entertaining. The story goes that R. Porter Ashe and Billy Wallace, both prominent San Francisco lawyers, shook dice for the lady's hand. Wallace won.

The bridal party departed by train from Sacramento for San Francisco, where the ceremony was to take place. En route Wallace left the coach for the smoking car. Ashe, also on board, saw his opportunity, seized it and persuaded the fickle charmer to get off and marry him in Martinez.

The couple had a daughter, Gladys, but they soon were divorced and Aimee whipped off to India. In a maharajah's palace in Bombay she acquired her second spouse, Harry Gillig, man-about-New York.

Harry was shed in court, too, and next came Jackson Gouraud, another New Yorker.

The pattern of marriage and divorce, suits and settlements was beginning to get monotonous. But Aimee didn't have to toss Jackson out. He died. So she turned to foreign fields and younger men. Next on her bridal path was the Russian "Prince" (there's some question about it) Alexander Miskinoff, many years her junior. She divorced him a few years later.

After virtuously asserting she was at last finished with romance—"The dew is off the rose. I am getting old and am content to worship at the feet of Buddha"—she had a change of heart. The wayword Crocker belle celebrated her 62nd birthday in 1925 with her marriage to another Russian prince—Alexander Galitzine—whose age was hers with the digits reversed. That union, too, concluded in the usual manner a couple of years later.

The prince had become sulky in double harness. He wanted to be a movie star.

Dudley Gunn, a San Franciscan who knew Aimee all of her life, has furnished some first-hand information about this tiger lily of the Edwardian era.

His first recollection is of Aimee at an early morning hour in full evening regalia driving a garbage truck home from a party.

He also recalls that a friend strolling past the Crocker home on Van Ness avenue one night noticed that the blinds weren't drawn and peered in. There sat the youthful Aimee perched atop an upright piano, playing the keys with her toes.

Aimee was inordinately fond of pearls ("they *say* something to me," she wrote "but I could not have told you what"). She also developed a fondness for snakes. Gunn maintained that she had replicas of the reptiles tattooed over much of her body.

He remembered having cocktails with her in Paris more than 50 years ago:

"She was wearing three strands of perfectly matched pink pearls the size of marbles. They kept dangling over the tattooed head of a reclining viper."

Mr. Gunn also recollected the time a pet boa constrictor four yards long and eight inches thick emerged from Aimee's room in a New York hotel and precipitated pandemonium until the fire department coaxed it back, with a cage of live rabbits as bait. Then it promptly ascended to the chandelier.

That errant slithery customer must have been Kaa, who belonged to the Princess Mara Davi, a bosom friend. Both of them took up residence with Aimee in Manhattan. Kaa doted on Davi and they slept together, the snake cozily coiled about her. He fancied Aimee, too, and one night snuck into her room, slid under the covers and encircled her.

Aimee didn't flick a muscle. In fact she relaxed them. Her comment: "It was like being in the strong embrace of a man."

A Matter of Honor

O N MORE than one occasion the serenity within the Pacific Union Club has been shattered by altercation.

John D. Spreckels, Sr. and a peppery little chap named Count F. de Jouffroy d'Abbans got into a fracas at the exclusive Nob Hill club in 1909. The august financier then was owner of the old morning *Call*, and the Count had been serving as secretary of the French Consulate here.

In the eight short months that the diplomat had been stationed in San Francisco he had made his presence felt in a variety of off-beat ways.

For one thing he had been tossed out of an Oakland hotel for speaking too loudly and thus disrupting a meeting of the Sons of the American Revolution.

He also had run afoul of the management of the Fairmont Hotel for not paying his bills, and at another time had exchanged blows with an automobile salesman.

All of these peccadillos had been reported in full detail in Spreckels' *Call*. The derogatory clippings had been sent to Washington, D.C., and Paris. Evidently the French Government thought it wise to recall its belligerent representative before he got into more serious trouble.

So, on the eve of his ignominious departure, the Count dropped in at the P.U. Club, where Spreckels was having lunch, and demanded that the latter print retractions. Spreckels promised nothing, but said that he would investigate the matter.

The Count said he intended to sue. However, if Spreckels could see his way clear to soothing his wounded feelings with $1000 he would be generous enough to depart without further ado.

The proposition smelled like a shakedown to the millionaire, who arose and roared that he wouldn't give the scamp a penny. It was then that d'Abbans drew himself up to his full five feet four inches and slapped Spreckels' face.

Confusion ensued. Spreckels, a handy man with his fists, insisted that he had let fly a couple of taps and knocked his adversary down. The Count countered that he had been seized by a flock of irate members who proceeded to beat him. Only the principals talked—everyone else clammed up.

But the nobleman left for France on schedule.

"I got my satisfaction with the slap," he told reporters—adding in a nice touch, "I was wearing my street gloves at the time."

Sherman's Return to San Francisco

AT THE beginning of 1853 the future Civil War hero, William Tecumseh Sherman, decided to return to California. He'd been here in the 1840s, and fought in the war with Mexico. Later he was assistant adjutant general to the U.S. military governor, Colonel Richard B. Mason, with whom he inspected the mines during the Gold Rush, and eventually sailed for the East in January, 1850.

Leaving the Army temporarily to engage in private business, he now was toying with the idea of settling in San Francisco and subsequently did become a partner in a local banking house.

He sailed from New Orleans for Nicaragua in February, 1853 with 600 other passengers—all but 60 of them men.

After an uneventful land-crossing to the Pacific, the travelers boarded the steamship *Lewis* and a terrific scramble for cabins ensued.

Sherman managed to get a berth in a choice outside cabin and was just about to leave the purser's window when an attractive blonde asked him to try to secure accommodations for herself and her female friend.

This he did—but the harassed officer assigned the women

to Sherman's stateroom. And he entered them on the passenger list as "Captain Sherman and ladies!" The women promptly moved in and Sherman moved out.

Finally he got another bunk. However, the women continued to be regarded as "his ladies" for the remainder of the trip and always were seated with him at meals.

Some time later a former fellow passenger asked Sherman how well he had known Mrs. D.—the flaxen-haired charmer who sang so sweetly and came out "under his special escort."

Sherman replied that the modest, well-behaved Mrs. D. was merely a chance acquaintance who was journeying to San Francisco to meet her beloved husband.

His informant snorted that she was a notorious "woman of the town."

As Sherman commented dryly in his reminiscences: "Society in California then was decidedly mixed."

Proceeding slowly north, the *Lewis* passed Monterey 18 days later, expecting to reach San Francisco before dawn on April 9. About four o'clock that morning Sherman was awakened by a bump and assumed that the ship had docked.

However the ship had bypassed the Golden Gate in a dense fog and had struck a reef off Bolinas and was stuck fast. The frightened passengers were near panic but fortunately the sea was relatively calm and there was no imminent danger of the ship breaking up.

A scouting party in one of the lifeboats ascertained that shore was less than a mile away and the systematic business of removing the travelers began with all the women and the "worse-scared" men going first.

Sherman, who was among the last to leave, had calmly whiled away the time munching on crackers and sardines which he'd found floating in the submerged pantry.

Once on land he and a young man set off to get help. They located some millhands who directed them to a schooner about to leave for San Francisco with a load of lumber. The captain, whose "crew" consisted of one 12-year-old boy, agreed to take the pair.

Within a couple of hours a stiff breeze was whisking them through the Golden Gate and smack into a strong ebb tide.

The schooner "dove like a duck," went over on her side, and Sherman was dunked in the Bay.

Someone at Fort Point saw the accident and rowed out to the rescue.

He hadn't been in the least alarmed, Sherman maintained, "but thought two shipwrecks in one day not a good beginning for a new, peaceful career."

The Undertaker Wouldn't Let Go

THE MOTIVATING force behind the "holdout," a person who hangs onto property by upping the asking price many times its value, is usually greed. Sometimes, the owner gets away with this brand of extortion.

At other times he may hoist himself on his own petard. Such was the case in the late '70s of Nicholas Yung, a San Francisco undertaker.

Railroad tycoon Charles Crocker had come down from Sacramento with the intention of erecting a mansion on Nob Hill as imposing as those which had been built by his partners, Collis P. Huntington and Leland Stanford, and the bonanza barons. He set about acquiring for the purpose the entire block bounded by California, Jones, Taylor and Sacramento streets, the present site of Grace Cathedral.

Yung owned a small house on a narrow lot fronting Sacramento street. Crocker offered him $3000 for it—a fair, if not fancy, price for the day. Yung doubled the ante and the millionaire balked.

However, when Crocker did come around, the mortician promptly tacked on another $3000. This cat-and-mouse game went on for quite a while. Some authorities estimate that the price went up to $12,000; others say as high as $30,000.

In any event, Crocker finally flipped, bared his teeth and told Yung to take a leap into the Bay of which he had such a fine view. He proceeded to spend $450,000 on a four-stories-high redwood woodcarver's delirium of bay windows, columns and pillars.

East and west were one-story ells containing drawing rooms and an art gallery. Surmounting the pile was a tower rising 76 feet above the sidewalk. The house faced on California street but was set well back.

The Yung cottage, of course, was dwarfed by the residence, but the embittered Crocker had no thought of stopping there. Despite the fact that it could have added nothing to the aesthetic value of the property, he ordered a 40-foot-high fence built around three sides of Yung's lot. It cut off all the light and most of the air.

As soon as the news of the impending spite fence got out, the townspeople began trudging up the hill to watch its progress and sidewalk superintendents by the hundreds gathered daily to jeer or cheer. The Board of Health was drawn into the act once on a vague sanitation basis, but backed away without doing anything.

The Yungs stuck it out for a couple of years. The undertaker made one nose-thumbing gesture by placing a product of his profession—a coffin embellished with skull and crossbones—on his roof plainly visible to anyone who might look out of the Crockers' rear windows. Then the Yungs gave up the struggle and had their house moved to a lot on Broderick street.

But by this time Crocker must have become attached to his fence, because when he died in 1897—20 years after its completion—the monstrosity still stood.

The Perils of Pauline

I N ROW 46 in the GAR plot at the Presidio's National Cemetery stands the usual simple white marker. But beneath the gravestone lie the remains of a most unusual person—an officer and a lady.

Engraved on the stark monument are the words "Pauline C. Fryer Union Spy."

Born Pauline Cushman in New Orleans in 1833, she later was taken to Grand Rapids, where her father ran a trading post. Pauline grew into a dark-eyed beauty. Tired of the crude life in the Michigan town, she decided to go on the stage and at 18 left for New York.

Though no Sarah Bernhardt, her vivid good looks, engaging personality and dashing manner soon won her an enthusiastic following among theater-goers.

Her popularity was at its peak when, in 1863, during the second year of the Civil War, she was playing in Louisville, Kentucky. The city already was under control of the Union forces, although the large number of Confederate captives apparently were permitted astonishing privileges, even being allowed to attend the theater.

After a performance one night, a Reb officer appeared in

Pauline's dressing room. He offered her $500 if sometime during the play she would propose a toast to Jefferson Davis and the Confederate army.

Pauline undoubtedly was shook up but she kept her cool and, after only a slight hesitation, agreed.

In less than an hour, however, she was closeted with the Union provost marshal, and before she emerged just prior to daybreak, they'd made a deal. With specific plans and instructions, Pauline had become a full-fledged spy for the North.

In the course of a supper scene in the play the next evening, she suddenly raised her glass and ad libbed the toast. Union sympathizers in the audience were shocked into silence. The Southerners, naturally, cheered.

Promptly booted out of the company for her disloyal act, Pauline headed south into Confederate territory, where she was received with open arms.

She quickly proved to be a brave and reliable agent, providing her superiors for the next several months with valuable information on troop movements, fortifications and locations of supplies and hospitals. Often she'd gallop on horseback in the dead of night across battle lines to deliver her data in person.

Her dramatic training came in handy as she'd been ordered to write nothing down. But the time came when she acquired so many details that she was afraid to trust her memory and broke the rule.

As luck would have it, she was captured, the written material found on her, and she was sentenced to hang. However, exhausted by her strenuous and dangerous role, Pauline fell ill, was hospitalized by the Rebs in Shelbyville and her punishment temporarily postponed.

Fortunately, the boys in blue took over before she recovered and the boys in gray decamped, leaving her behind.

Hailed as a heroine, she was commissioned a brevet major and given a uniform.

Love in the person of Charles Dickinson had come into her life before the war was over. She married him, retired, and they settled in Michigan, which Pauline had left for New York while still in her teens.

Dickinson was a musician and presumably not a prosperous one. For by the early '70s, when she was approaching 40, Pauline went back on the stage.

Her tours took her to the West Coast, and she appeared at San Francisco's Metropolitan Theater around 1872.

By then there were seven little Dickinsons to feed and clothe!

Dire, dramatic events were lurking in the wings, however.

Diphtheria carried off four of her children in a single day. A few days later, the remaining three also succumbed to the dread disease.

Within a short time, too, her husband died.

According to some historians, Pauline subsequently married a man named August Tichner, but we've been unable to run down details on that union.

At any rate, her last spouse was Jerry Fryer, a sheriff in Pinole county, Arizona. It must be assumed that this marriage was not a happy one, for she soon left him, and sometime during the late '80s came to San Francisco.

She was a competent, though never a great actress. Much of her theatrical success had depended on her youthful beauty and bounce. Now her career was over.

She managed to live on her Army pension, augmented by meager royalties from an autobiography she'd written and fees from occasional lectures given before historical societies and patriotic organizations.

Then, on a December day in 1893, the landlady of a rooming house on Market street, where Pauline, now 60, alone and ill, had occupied a small third-story room, found her lying unconscious on the floor.

Four hours later she was dead.

Suicide? Possibly, and yet . . .

Although several dolorous poems penned by Pauline were found in her room, there also were a few reasonably cheerful letters, one even discussing a trip to Texas she was planning.

The verdict of the coroner's jury was that she had died of an accidental overdose of morphine taken, conceivably, to relieve the pain of sciatic rheumatism.

"Cushman," the name by which she had become famous, appears only as the letter "C" on her tombstone.

Worse — through some inexplicable error which went uncorrected for more than a half-century, her married name originally was misspelled and chiselled "Tyer" into the marker.

Death Called Charley's Bluff

ONE OF the toughest, most daring and capable stage drivers West of the Rockies during the middle of the last century was a character known as "One-Eyed" (sometimes "Cock-Eyed") Charley Parkhurst.

His fame for pluck and recklessness spread with every passenger he took careening over dusty or muddy roads on runs from San Francisco or Oakland to San Jose and Santa Cruz, from Stockton to Placerville, or wherever.

Despite his prowess he was no more than 5 feet 6 inches tall. His comparatively small hands, on which he habitually wore embroidered gauntlets, nevertheless handled a six-horse team with consummate skill.

His beardless face was deeply sunburnt and usually stained about the mouth and chin with tobacco juice.

He'd lost the sight of his left eye, after he was accidentally kicked by a horse and wore a patch over it, which added to his raffish appearance and accounted for his nickname.

When the occasion called for it, as it often did, he'd swear like a trooper in a rather high-pitched voice. He smoked two-bit cigars and chewed continuously, drank in moderation and played poker with the boys, although he was something of a loner and showed no interest in women.

Stories of Charley's exploits were told with awe and relish. There was the time, for instance, he'd driven his horses across a rickety bridge over the swollen Tuolumne River in a blinding rainstorm. No sooner had the stage reached the other side than the bridge swayed crazily and collapsed.

Around 1858 Charley, constantly plagued by rheumatism, retired from the rugged routine and opened a stage station and saloon on 25 acres he'd bought near Soquel between Santa Cruz and Watsonville. Later he raised cattle in a small way, but after he could no longer sit in a saddle, he operated a little chicken ranch in the vicinity of Aptos.

Finally in 1876 he sold the place to a neighboring farmer friend and moved into a cabin on the property. There, three years later, he died alone of cancer of the mouth, three days after Christmas.

Undertakers preparing the body for burial made the astonishing discovery that this person who'd lived like a man was really a woman! Moreover, a doctor maintained that she had been a mother.

Born in New Hampshire in 1812, according to some historians, she had been christened Charlotte. At any rate, as a youngster she ran away from an orphanage, and wearing boy's clothes and short-cut hair got a job in a stable, where she learned to care for horses and to drive.

When the stable owner came to California to establish a stage line, he brought this fine young employee along.

She rests in the old Pioneer Cemetery in Watsonville. Engraved on the tombstone, however, is the name "Charley Darkey Parkhurst, noted whip of the Gold Rush Days . . ."

Together in Life and Death

T HE NEXT time you visit the University of California Medical School take a good long look at the bust of Dr. Hugh Huger Toland in the lobby, or his portrait hanging in the building's auditorium.

For here was a man who it is said kept his deceased wife in a glass-topped coffin in his office for 25 years!

Much has been written about the achievements of this brilliant physician and surgeon, who, in 1864, founded the Toland Medical School in North Beach, the forerunner of today's extensive, renowned medical complex on Parnassus Heights. But the fascinating facet of his life concerning his late wife is not to be found in most of the pioneer doctor's biographies.

Dr. Toland already was a wealthy and prominent citizen of Columbia, South Carolina, and a widower when he first met lovely 21-year-old Mary America Avery at her debut ball in that city.

A serious man of Scottish-Irish ancestry, he stood well over six feet, had jet black hair, piercing blue eyes and a jutting, determined jaw.

He was immediately smitten by the girl's great beauty and, despite the disparity in their ages, they were married following a whirlwind courtship.

There were several reasons why Dr. Toland decided to come to California. For one thing, gold had been discovered. Then he foresaw that war between the Northern and Southern States was inevitable. Furthermore, as his bride was almost as delicate as she was delectable, he thought a change of climate might improve her health.

So they set off, the doctor first promising Mary America's mother that, should any ill befall her daughter, he'd return her.

No expense was spared in travel arrangements. Mary America's brother, Dr. E. T. Avery, was in the caravan that traveled at a leisurely pace for some six months across the continent.

Then on a September night in 1852 the party made camp a few miles from San Francisco in an area that, unknown to them, was infected with cholera. Mary America contracted the dread disease and died three days later. Her husband took the body to this city and had it embalmed under his direction.

Dr. Toland felt responsible for his bride's death and his racking, painful grief etched deeply into his stern face.

Eight years later he married another Mary, a poetess of note. This remarkable woman presumably was free from jealousy and apparently never objected to the continued presence of her predecessor, cold in her casket though she was.

A short time before he died in 1880 Dr. Toland recalled the promise he had made to Mary America's mother and took her back to South Carolina where she was buried in a cemetery at Ebenezer. (The third Mrs. Toland graciously accompanied him on the trip.)

The epitaph on her grave reads:
"No one so beautiful as she,
"Fairest of form and face,
"A queenly mien with modesty,
"Crowned in every other grace."

A Disappearing Rebel

SAN FRANCISCO, it seems, always has nurtured a collection of colorful, controversial members of the bar.

But none of the current crop can top a brilliant, if erratic, early day local lawyer named Rufus A. Lockwood — although there are a few around who conceivably might have given him competition.

Like a number of lawyers today, he managed to grab plenty of publicity in his time.

But, unlike his modern counterparts, Lockwood cared nothing for money, and, moreover, periodically chucked his profession, sometimes after pulling off a spectacular coup.

An unpredictable social rebel, he also had a propensity for disappearing periodically, a practice that produced gaps in his history.

Lockwood was born Jonathan Jessup in Stamford, Connecticut, in 1811, and at the age of 18 entered Yale, where he remained for a year before leaving to join the Navy.

So indignant was he when a shipmate was flogged for some minor infraction during a cruise to the Caribbean, that he promptly deserted.

This possibly accounts for the fact that he adopted his

mother's maiden name and changed his first name as well.

Anyhow, he worked his way to Chicago and eventually settled in Indiana, taught school there and began to study law.

In that era, requirements for the bar were more relaxed than now, and by 1834 he was admitted to practice before that state's Supreme Court.

He argued his first case in Lafayette so expertly that he received the commendation of the justices.

The following year he defended a client in a sensational murder trial and won an acquittal after talking for nine hours straight!

His colleagues enthusiastically pronounced it the best jury speech ever made on this or any other continent.

Now comes one of the diffused chapters. Lockwood went broke, then somehow got to Mexico where he studied Spanish law, became ill and returned to this country—still minus funds.

In New Orleans he enlisted in the Army in order to raise $20 to redeem his suitcase from a pawnbroker.

An influential friend arranged his discharge and financed a trip back to Lafayette, where he resumed his career.

He soon took a case and argued eloquently for three days against the admission of a will to probate. When the verdict went against him, he was so infuriated and disgusted that he vowed never to practice again.

This was in 1849 and, naturally enough, Lockwood decided to go to California and look for gold. He left all his law books behind and employed himself studying medicine during the long voyage around The Horn.

He never prescribed a pill, or picked up a shovel either. After a brief stay in Mission San Jose he came to San Francisco, and in short order was one of the best known lawyers in the State.

"An awkward bear of a man" is the way some described Lockwood. Others said that he resembled "an old lion at play."

All agree, however, that he was tall, husky and ungainly

with broad shoulders and a face marked by high cheek bones and penetrating gray-blue eyes.

There is no question either about his brilliance and capriciousness, nor any doubts about his fondness for drink, and his propensity for gambling and for frequently going AWOL.

Lockwood took a job in the law office of Horace Hawes, another able but erratic character. It was as clerk and janitor for a daily pittance, which he consistently blew on the roulette tables.

A couple of years later, though, he resumed his profession in earnest, affiliating with two eminent and successful pioneer attorneys—Edmund Randolph, one of *the* Randolphs of Virginia, and Frank Tilford of Kentucky. They made a formidable and respected trio.

At one point Lockwood, bucking the powerful and popular forces of the Vigilante Committee, won an important case and his fame spread.

But no sooner had he achieved acclaim than he abruptly withdrew from the partnership and went to work on the waterfront as a stevedore.

Apparently the business of lifting loads and toting bales soon palled. So when he was offered the post of chief counsel for a big, prosperous banking firm in the city, he took it.

Lockwood began to make a lot of money, too, but couldn't keep it in his pockets. It's said that he occasionally got his kicks by skipping $20 gold pieces across the waters of the Bay from the end of Meiggs' Wharf.

Somewhere along the line he had married and fathered children. In 1853, being in the chips, he sent for his family to join him in San Francisco, then promptly departed for Australia. (Mrs. L. must have been the most meek and understanding spouse ever to enter the bonds of matrimony.)

He remained Down Under for two years earning his way as a sheepherder, clerk and bookkeeper. Whatever else may have happened is a minor mystery, but the fact remains that when he returned he was strangely mellowed and appeared considerably chastened. He gave up gambling, for instance, and embraced the Roman Catholic faith.

Then in 1857, he decided to take a trip East and, with his spouse and four children, sailed in September.

Three days out of Havana, they ran into a terrible storm. The ship was in serious danger and all able-bodied men were ordered to man the pumps.

Lockwood diligently did his duty for a while but then became bored with the arduous task. Two tales are told about what happened next.

One yarn goes that he said "To hell with this stuff," retired to his stateroom and calmly began to read a book. The other maintains that he merely lit a cigar and sat on the deck smoking until the end came.

In any event, he went down with several hundred other passengers. His wife, however, was rescued.

This long-suffering lady, used to his periodic absences, often said later that any day she fully expected him to knock on the door.

But this time Lockwood, now 46, had disappeared permanently.

Oscar Wasn't Wild About San Francisco

Oscar Wilde was not wild about San Francisco—and vice versa. The reaction possibly stemmed from disappointment on both sides.

For some inexplicable reason, although the 26-year-old Irish poet-playwright-wit had scheduled only a single lecture in New York and made one-night stands elsewhere during his 1882 tour three talks were slated for San Francisco.

Wilde held ideas far advanced for his era and revolted against most things Victorian, ranging from morality to modes in dress, decor and architecture. So not only San Francisco but all of America was to reverberate under his broadsides.

And there's no denying he was as eccentric as he was aesthetic.

Wilde's arrival in San Francisco, only 30 years removed from boisterous boomtown days and pretty self-conscious about it, was greatly anticipated and generated much excitement.

Devotees along the route West had pressed floral offerings on him. He'd tenderly nursed across the continent a box of violets someone in New York had given him, for instance, as well as a camellia from Reno, sunflowers in Sacramento, and even a pansy an admirer had thrust into his hand in Benicia.

A welcoming committee composed of several Bohemian Club members, a clutch of reporters and his local agent went to Port Costa to board his train and ride to Oakland with him. The meeting was hardly of the hearty, backslapping type.

In fact, one of the two managers traveling with Wilde (his entourage also included a valet to look after his six trunks and collection of objets d'art) hushed the visitors, explaining that Wilde was paying his morning devotion to the camellia.

When he joined the group his appearance was more exotic than reassuring. Boyish, but heavy featured, he had brown locks that hung to his shoulders.

He had on dark brown trousers, a rose-colored tie and a sunflower sprouted from the lapel of his brown velvet jacket.

Wilde admired the scenery from the top deck of a ferry boat as he crossed the Bay, but recoiled at the "ghastly waterfront smells," stuck his nose into the camellia and was still smelling it when his carriage whisked him off to the Palace Hotel.

Platt's Hall on Montgomery street was filled to overflowing when Oscar Wilde gave the first of his three lectures.

The women, many of whom undoubtedly had dragged their husbands behind them to this cultural feast, rustled in their most gorgeous gowns and flashed their best diamonds.

The renowned man of letters, they felt, certainly would be impressed by the chic and sophisticated assemblage and they in turn were prepared to be duly impressed by him.

On the stage had been placed a black lectern with art objects from the poet-playwright's own collection set in the niches. On it was a vase holding a single lily.

The audience had had plenty of time to contemplate the posy, too, as it was 9:20 before the lion of the evening loped in for his 8 o'clock lecture.

Lace frothed from the cuffs of his black velvet coat, and an antique jeweled pin glittered in his flowing lace jabot.

He wore black velvet knee breeches and white gloves and his long hair was brushed back over his ears.

The chattering crew fell into stunned silence as Wilde took his place and stared at them coldly.

Things didn't improve when he began to talk.

His delivery was a dreary monotone, and his British accent was so pronounced that he was difficult to understand.

But as he progressed the listeners became more used to his manner of speech and began to get the drift.

In the beginning the gist had been to the general effect that true art couldn't exist without craftsmanship and vice versa.

Then he got down to specifics.

Wilde lambasted the ladies who insisted upon painting and embellishing everything in sight from soup plates to bathroom fixtures.

He sneered at the city's houses, calling them "dreary, utterly, inexpressibly hideous."

Looking pointedly at the audience, he proclaimed the garb of the fashionably dressed American "barbaric and vulgar."

Thus he spoke for about 45 minutes before ambling off the stage.

The following nights the outraged smart set stayed away in droves.

His subject was "Art in Decoration," and although he made much sense he made no more of a hit with the "Jessie street milliners and Minna street seamstresses" than he had with the creme de la creme.

Traveling through America had been a depressing experience, he declared—the air polluted with smoke and grime, the architecture depraved.

He recommended that houses be built of stone and marble or, if of wood, then hand-carved. Cast-iron railings he regarded as repugnant; they should be hand-hammered. And so forth.

A tremor of disgust quivered through his ample frame as he recalled the monstrous American hatracks. When he started on women's ridiculous bonnets, half the audience left.

Wilde's activities during his San Francisco visit were not confined to the three less than scintillating lectures.

In her memoirs, Aimee Crocker mentions that at a party she gave, he drank everyone under the table, switched from whiskey to gin at 3 a.m. and insisted on continuing the festivities.

In fact, among the more lasting impressions the author left behind, seems to have been a healthy respect for his fortitude and the liquor he could hold.

One story goes that upon entering the Bohemian Club, where he'd been invited to dine by a group of members, he plunked himself into the most comfortable chair and immediately called for strong cigars and absinthe.

By dawn most of the hosts had folded or vanished, but the poet was still rarin' to go and asked if there wasn't "another gay place of entertainment in this city."

There were no regrets when Wilde, his two managers, valet, half a dozen trunks and collection of objets d'art left San Francisco.

It may be considered significant, however, that a number of groups and clubs dedicated to the study of decorative arts soon sprang up.

As a final note, it seems that his declaration of his objets d'art had not entirely satisfied the U.S. Customs officials in New York.

But as he was making one-night stands across the nation,

they couldn't question him until he finally lighted in San Francisco.

When asked if he had omitted to declare anything upon entry into this country, Wilde supposedly answered:

"Only my genius."

He Lived Like a Prince

EVALYN WALSH MCLEAN spent the winter of 1914 in Florida, where she had chartered a yacht.

Recalling those days in her autobiography, "Father Struck It Rich," the late famed Washington hostess and long-time owner of the Hope Diamond tells the beginning of a winter-spring tale.

"One of our acquaintances at Palm Beach was old Mrs. William Rhinelander Stewart, who by this time was the widow of James Henry (Silent) Smith," wrote the author.

"She was past 60 and all her life had been accumulating jewelry.

"Tiffany might have started a branch with what she wore even when she was going swimming.

"One day there appeared on the most exclusive section of the beach a young fellow in a pale pink bathing suit, a pretty good imitation of flesh color. He was strolling with a white and gray Russian wolfhound."

Quite boldly he was making eyes at this old woman, and his eyes were big and fringed with long lashes. He got a quick response from the elderly widow.

"Under her breath she said to me intensely: 'Meet this fellow and invite us both aboard the *Bluebird*.' "

That picturesque fellow was Jean de St. Cyr, subsequently a familiar figure in San Francisco society.

Later, after someone had presented him to her, Mrs. McLean did ask him to a dinner party on the yacht, including among other guests the smitten Mrs. Smith.

"This strange young man was so much younger than her son, Willie Stewart Jr., that her interest in him might have seemed at first glance to be maternal," the writer continued.

"But I saw her arrange the yachting cap on his dark curly hair . . . and let a jeweled finger scrape his ear. That very minute I was sorry I had introduced them.

"Willie and I did all we could to break it up, but we had no chance — what glittered in his mother's eyes was something that 35 years before could have been called girlish love."

In any event, de St. Cyr and the aging Mrs. Smith were married a few months later and came to San Francisco on their honeymoon.

Mrs. Smith's social position had been exalted in her native Baltimore, and equally so in New York as the wife of William Rhinelander Stewart, whom she'd married in 1879.

It had not been weakened by their subsequent divorce or her marriage a few days later to James Henry (Silent) Smith, known as the enigma of Wall street.

(The latter union was short-lived. He died in Japan on their wedding trip, leaving her all his millions.)

But the elite couldn't quite cotton to her latest acquisition.

Rumor was strong that the young man, supposedly stemming from an aristocratic French family, actually was plain Jack Thompson of Texas.

Also that previous to espousing his first wealthy widow, who left him a cool million, he'd worked as a clerk in hotels and department stores, as a waiter and chorus boy.

Moreover, the fancy attire he affected—lavender-lined suits,

butterfly-embroidered socks, black-laced white shoes, etc.—
offended his wife's Social Register friends.

So in 1919, less than four years after their simple and secret
marriage at White Sulphur Springs, West Virginia, the couple
came back to California.

She bought "El Cerrito," the elegant San Mateo showplace
that had belonged to Eugene de Sabla, a local banker, and
spent thousands furnishing the mansion and making improvements.

Soon afterward, Mrs. de St. Cyr deeded the estate over to
her husband.

They found the social climate here much more agreeable.

It was in the handsome house on the Peninsula property
that she died in 1925.

Her will stipulated that her fortune, which ran in the pleasant neighborhood of $20 to $30 millions, should be divided
among her two children and her helpmate.

So Jean de St. Cyr, whom friends in San Francisco always—
and probably appropriately enough—called "Rex," continued
to reign over and entertain in his domain for almost another
15 years.

Long gone by this time was the flamboyant raiment de St.
Cyr had affected in his salad days, and his 35-room residence
was a model of exquisite furnishings and appointments.

Moreover, he was a popular extra man in local society.
There had been periodic rumors of remarriage but it wasn't
until April, 1939, that he stunned society by galloping down
the bridal path for the third time.

His partner at this point was the widow of George Carter,
former governor of Hawaii, mother of Mrs. Douglas Alexander
of Burlingame and — need it be said? — rich.

Friends received still another shock, combined with perplex-
ity, the very next month when they learned that he'd sold

"El Cerrito" for $400,000 to his bride, who, incidentally, already owned a showplace in Honolulu.

It soon became evident that this union wasn't destined for longevity, although for a while the frequently separated couple indignantly denied divorce rumors.

Nevertheless, in January of the following year the third Mrs. de St. Cyr, ill and declining, filed suit in Reno, got her freedom in February, and put "El Cerrito" on the market in March.

All the mansion's furnishings were sold at six auction sessions that same month. The peak day throng, estimated at 6000 people, turned the event into a nightmare for a harassed corps of guides and guards.

But an enterprising soft drink salesman made a neat profit by setting up a stand near one entrance!

By this time de St. Cyr had moved to Southern California where he lived out his last days.

The Lavender Man

FOR THOUSANDS of San Franciscans during nearly half a century the perfume of lavender was as much a part of the Christmas season's aroma as the smell of popcorn and greenery.

They caught whiffs of it deliciously scenting the air around the Emporium as they dashed back and forth along Market street on shopping expeditions.

Countless numbers paused in their hectic pace to exchange holiday greetings with the pleasant man who sold it and to spend a dime or two for a couple of packets to take home.

The vendor was Anthony Barrett, who had come to this country around the hinge of the century to seek his fortune and found employment in mines in Arizona.

Tragedy struck in 1905. There was an explosion and Tony was blinded in the accident. He came here for treatment but his sight was gone forever.

No one would hire the young man, and he was becoming desperate when he remembered that in his youth packages of the old-fashioned fragrance used to sell very well on the streets in England.

So he bought some lavender, put it into simple paper wrappers, displayed them on a tray suspended from straps around his shoulders and took a stand (in later years he sat) at the west entrance to the Emporium.

There he was to remain—a living landmark—for the next 45 years.

Tony always was quiet. He didn't hawk his wares or in any other way try to attract customers.

Nevertheless, he managed to make a meager living and a wealth of friends.

Eventually the department store's management built him a little shelter against the chill winds and damp fogs, and thus he became almost a part of that institution.

One day in the early 1950s Tony was missing. During a three-year illness he always was hopeful of returning to his post and fretted at the delay.

But Tony died, aged 73, in the spring of 1955 at the Laguna Honda Home.

With his death the city lost one of its best-known but gentlest characters, and the newspapers afforded him obituaries of a length usually reserved for bank presidents.

No monument that might mark his grave in Holy Cross Cemetery could be more enduring or endearing than the nostalgic memory of the sweet scent of lavender he left behind.

Drama in the Garden Court

THE ONCE brilliant sun of the silent screen star, Mae Murray, already had set when she arrived in the mid-1950s and registered at San Francisco's Palace Hotel.

Despite a somewhat seedy appearance she still had the airs and graces of a reigning queen and expected to be treated with the reverence due such.

That evening she turned up in the Garden Court for dinner wearing a simple black dress cut low in the neckline and her trademark—a large black hat trimmed with a plume atop her fluffy blonde curls.

But as a perverse fate would have it, this was the opening night of the opera season.

The court was jammed with elegantly attired opera-bound guests, and only those in evening clothes were permitted.

Miss Murray explained that she hadn't brought an evening gown with her. But rules were rules.

How could the management extricate itself from this sticky wicket without offending? Obviously it was a job for public relations.

So someone hastily summoned Lucy Nunes who then headed that department at the Palace.

She proved equal to the delicate situation and immediately went into high gear.

First she rounded up a contingent of the hotel's junior executives (most of whom had never even heard of La Murray), shepherded them with the petite performer into the bar and ordered champagne for all hands.

Next she had a tense conversation with the venerable headwaiter, who *did* remember the star in her prime.

He ordered a small table put up under a sheltering palm in a remote corner of the room.

Thus the regulations were not broken—merely bent a bit.

Then Lucy remembered that a prominent newspaperwoman, vacationing from her duties in Ohio, was staying at the hotel.

She begged her to join Miss Murray with pad and pencil and do an interview. The lady agreed.

Alerted, too, was the orchestra leader.

As he led the "Merry Widow Waltz," theme song for her greatest film triumph, a soft spotlight from the rim of the court's roof bathed the actress in a flattering glow.

The effect was almost miraculous. Erased were the ravages wrought by time. Magically restored was much of the glamor of her youth.

Miss Murray beamed and bowed with regal dignity.

The other diners, following the shaft of light, stared at the little woman in black. But, alas, there were no signs of recognition, no applause.

The awful moment seemed to hang taut, suspended in time.

Then a courtly, elderly gentleman in white tie and tails rose from his table, walked to hers and kissed the hand she extended to him.

"I shall never forget how lovely you were the first time I saw you, my dear," he murmured, adding gently, "—as lovely as you are tonight."

It was the late Cotillion director Percy King who saved the day . . . and this gesture alone should insure him an especially bright jewel in his crown.

Index